Best Pub Walks in Leicestershire and Rutland

Chris Robson

Published by Sigma Leisure – an imprint of
Sigma Press, 1 South Oak Lane, Wilmslow, Cheshire SK9 6AR, England.

British Library Cataloguing in Publication Data
A CIP record for this book is available from the British Library.

ISBN: 1-85058-365-X

Typesetting and Design by: Sigma Press, Wilmslow, Cheshire.

Text photographs: The author and Chris Rushton

Cover photograph: The Curzon Arms, Woodhouse Eaves (Chris Rushton)

Printed by: Manchester Free Press

General Disclaimer

PREFACE

Leicestershire is located at the centre of England, and in many ways can be thought of as the Heart of the Shires. It exudes the very essence of traditional Englishness, with its picturebook villages and unspoilt countryside, yet at the same time at its heart is one of the most cosmopolitan cities in the country, Leicester.

To the outsider it is largely unknown, except perhaps as a series of junctions as they speed up the M1 to the more dramatic scenery of the north. Naming a famous person or place in Leicestershire is akin to the old teaser of finding well-known Belgians. It is a county without extremes of height, rising only to 912 feet, but it does have striking hills and is seldom uninteresting to walk.

Highlights include Charnwood and Rutland; if you do not know why these places are special then go and find out. You will not be disappointed. Take your time too. Whilst compiling these walks I found that I travelled at about two-thirds of my normal walking pace; not because it was difficult, which it certainly is not, but because there was so much to look at in the villages through which I passed. It has subtle scenery, more Mozart than Guns 'n' Roses, but it provides memorable days out. A bit like the Cotswolds, but without the tourists.

This book is about combining two of life's finest pleasures. I have often been asked whether the walk or the pub was chosen first; the answer is a mixture of the two. Some walks were designed to include a favourite pub, one or two were abandoned due to the lack of real ale or, in my opinion, a decent pub, and the odd one was rerouted to include a better pub when it was found. The initial planning involved reading books about the county, picking out interesting stories and features, marking them on the map and then looking for the best paths and roads to link them together. These would then be walked, with alterations made if there were difficulties on the ground or if something nearby looked too interesting to leave out.

I hope that you get as much pleasure out of these walks as I have, and find the historical notes informative and entertaining. My thanks to my wife Yvonne and mother Muriel for their company and advice on many of the walks, and to Lesley for her assistance with the text.

Chris Robson

Contents

INTRODUCTION

THE WALKS

LOCATION MAP

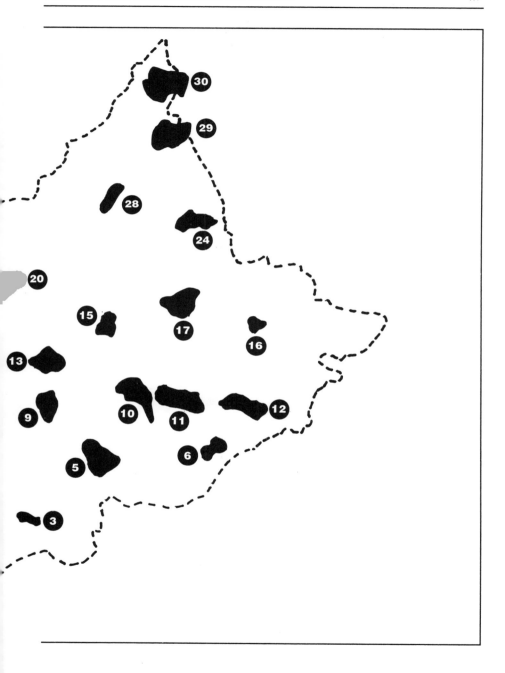

INTRODUCTION

The 30 circular walks in this book vary between 3.7 and 10 miles in length, with the majority in the 6 or 7 mile range. There are short walks for families or those long summer evenings, whilst the more adventurous will find it quite possible to encompass two walks on the same day. You may walk them backwards, though not literally I hope, run them, change the route or even sit in the pub while others do the hard work. However you tackle them, you will find plenty of interest to stimulate the conversation in the watering hole.

About Walking

In summer, many of these walks can be completed in suitable shoes or trainers, but beware of the rutted ground on some of the bridleways. Boots are virtually essential at other times, and please respect the publicans by removing boots or at least getting the mud off them before entering the bar. Do not forget your waterproofs and an extra sweater, and take more food than you think that you will need in case the walk takes longer than expected.

Always carry a map. The O.S. Landranger 1:50,000 series will be adequate, although the 1:25,000 Pathfinder series gives more detail and is useful for planning alternative routes. All walks have been checked for right of way, and any deviations mentioned in the text. It is your right to follow the paths as they are drawn on the map, but it is sensible to go around the edges of crop fields in summer if that is the locally accepted route and no path is maintained across the field. Since many routes were walked in winter there may be some problems with the routes that were not apparent at the time. If there are serious difficulties get around them as best you can and then contact the footpaths officers at Leicestershire County Council on 0533 323232.

Although every effort has been made to remove errors, there are still two sources of misdirection as you follow the book. Firstly there is the difference between your perception and mine. The obvious way to me along a green lane may not seem as noticeable to you as the tractor path branching left. It is easy to be engaged in conversation and without thinking take the wrong route. Should this happen then retrace your steps until you are certain that you are on the right route again and then look closely for the points mentioned in the text. Remember that my muddy lane may now be dry and vice-versa. It is also possible that since I knew in which direction I was heading I have missed some feature that is very obvious to you. I fully expect to be cursed on the odd occasion.

The second source of error is the changing nature of the countryside. Fences, walls, buildings and even woods can change. On one walk I was slightly thrown to discover a new road not marked on my map, which caused me to doubt my navigation for a minute. Such changes should not lead to any real problems, but it should be borne in mind that the prominent tree in the text may be the pile of logs on the ground.

Finally I should mention Waymark 2000, the scheme whereby Leicestershire County Council plan to mark every footpath and bridlepath in the county with the yellow posts and where appropriate new stiles, by the end of this century. This project means that many of the walks that I describe as being difficult in parts for route finding may well be much simpler when you meet them. At the time of writing work is in progress in the Burrough Hill area, which should alleviate the minor route problems on that walk. I have also brought to their attention the other walks that need work done on them, particularly Preston and Shackerstone, so hopefully life will be a little easier for you than it was for me. And of course you have an excellent guide book ...

The Public Houses

Beer and walking go well together, although the former can have a disastrous effect on the latter. Nevertheless the post-ramble tipple has been enjoyed for centuries, and catering for the traveller is the main reason for the existence of several of the pubs in this book. Although many pubs were also designed with the needs of the local population in mind, the decline in the rural population together with a massive increase in car ownership has seen a change in their role over the last 25 years. Now almost all serve a high standard of food and many have a restaurant attached.

The pubs in this book are some of the finest in the country, many being buildings of charm and antiquity. All serve real ale, a legacy that owes much to CAMRA, the campaign for real ale, which has championed the cause of the drinker for some 25 years. Those wishing to join should contact CAMRA at 34, Alma Road, St Albans, Herts, AL1 3BW. The variety of beers on offer has radically altered in the last few years, and the recent laws on ownership by breweries are having a great effect on not only the range of ales but also the very existence of some pubs. The consequence is that you can currently enjoy beers from all over the country as many inns have a variable guest beer, and I encountered over 60 different ales on my travels. The local Everard's, whose Tiger is amongst the best, and Ruddles will be much in evidence, as will the wide-ranging Marston's Pedigree and Boddington's. One home brew pub, the Parish Brewery at Somerby, will also be met.

The details about beers, food and opening times were provided by the pubs and correct at the time of publication. However these things do alter, particularly if there is a change of ownership, and so it is wise to check if it is likely to be important. If you were depending on the pub for Sunday dinner then it may well be sensible to book beforehand.

Most publicans welcome children, but occasionally they are not allowed inside. Children under the age of 14 are not legally allowed in bars, although if they are eating then it is usually fine. Many pubs now have special family rooms, but if not a quiet word with the landlord should help prevent any misunderstandings.

Transport

Most walks are accessible by bus or train, leaving you free to avoid the dilemma as to who will drive. I have indicated the numbers and frequency of service, but in this age of deregulation country buses are very vulnerable. In any case you will need to know details of times, so make sure that you either get hold of the individual timetables or phone the Busline on Leicester 313391.

Leicestershire County Council publishes a twice-yearly booklet listing all the transport routes and their frequencies, together with a detailed county map and town maps. It is excellent and served as my bible for getting about, copies being available in libraries, tourist offices and main bus stations.

Using public transport can enhance the day out, as you see far more from a bus than a car and the children will love it. No worries about breathalysers, and remember that it was in Leicester that the first Traffic Wardens appeared.

History

The oldest inhabitant was *Ceteosaurus*, a dinosaur who died 175 million years ago near Great Casterton and can now be seen in a Leicester museum. Man has left traces since the Bronze Age, back to about 1800 BC, with burial mounds and the spectacular hill-forts at Burrough Hill and Breedon. Leicester takes its name from Kaerleir, which according to the 12th century Geoffrey of Monmouth was a city ruled by King Leir in the 9th century BC. Shakespeare used Leir as the basis for King Lear, although no trace of Leir has ever been found.

More substantial evidence of habitation appears after the Roman Invasion in 43 AD, and the Jewry Wall Museum in Leicester, or Ratae as it was then known, displays remains from that period. The central location of Leicestershire accounts for its growth, with the Fosse Way channelling the movement of goods and people through it. At High Cross you get the chance to find out more about the road and how it was built.

The majority of Leicestershire villages were founded between 700 and 1066, the period of first Anglo-Saxon rule and then Danish dominance. The Saxon villages can be traced by their ending in *-ham*, *-ton* and *-worth*, whilst the Danish are *-by* and *-thorpe*. The Danes also gave us the word *-gate* for "street" or "way" which is commonly seen in the old parts of the villages. The Norman Conquest brought a time of stability and growth, with the building of Oakham, Belvoir and Leicester Castles. Oakham is well worth a visit for the Great Hall and its unique collection of horseshoes which were demanded from any peer of the land passing through.

The next figure of historical note was the 13th century Simon de Montfort, after whom the new university in Leicester is named, leader of the revolt against Edward III before he was defeated at Evesham. Simon's reputation as a "democrat" is perhaps a little misplaced, but he certainly was backed by the common man rather than the barons and landowners.

Leicester grew in importance, with Parliament being held there three times in the 15th century, but it is for the Battle of Bosworth Field and the death of King Richard III that the county is best remembered. More information can be found in the Market Bosworth walk.

Life under the Tudors saw the death of Cardinal Wolsey at St Mary's Abbey, Leicester, as he travelled to see King Henry VIII. The famous local hosiery company took his name as a tribute. Lady Jane Grey sadly became a pawn in Dudley's power-broking, a fuller description of which is in the Swithland walk, and the market towns of Loughborough, Melton, Hinckley, Oakham and Uppingham all grew and prospered.

During the Civil War Leicestershire was mainly Parliamentarian, but the city itself was captured by Prince Rupert for the King in 1645. However his defeat a month later at Naseby saw him fleeing northwards, pausing at Wistow to change horses, before going on to Ashby. Leicester was left in a poor state, but it was revived by the growth of the hosiery industry in the late 17th century.

The countryside was changing, and in the 18th century the better roads and canal building increased the prosperity of the towns. The enclosure of the old open fields accelerated, some 40% of the county being so altered between 1760 and 1800, leading to the pattern of large fields, hedges and ditches now apparent and so conducive to hunting. This led to the removal of small spinneys and the growth of new covets for the foxes and gamebirds to breed in. Great strides were made in stock breeding by Bakewell of Dishley and Paget of Ibstock, their work attracting interest throughout the world and ensuring Leicestershire of a place in the history of the agrarian revolution. The applications to the breeding of foxhounds were much appreciated locally.

The industrial revolution sparked a need for coal, and the development of the railways enabled the mines to satisfy the demands. Boot and shoe manufacturing took over from hosiery as the leading employer, whilst towns such as Coalville and Shepshed increased dramatically in size. More recently increased mechanisation in farming has reduced the rural population, which is now increasingly made up of commuters taking advantage of the growth of the road system.

Geography

On a simplistic level you can consider Leicestershire to be divided into two parts by the almost central River Soar. To the west are the claylands, giving rise to brick-built towns and industry, whilst to the east are the stone-based farmlands with their immaculate ironstone villages. Yet within each part of this bisection lie several subdivisions – Charnwood is a unique volcanic landscape and in stark contrast to the neighbouring coalfields and farmland, whilst the escarpments above Melton and Belvoir are not repeated in the rippling, rounded, Rutland countryside.

The north-west consists of alternating sandstones, ironstones, clay and coal. It is mainly farmland, with the coalfield based towns sprouting minor industries. Charnwood Forest has ancient rocks of granite thrusting through a covering mantle of fertile soil, an area of about 30 square miles which has lost most of the woodland. Here heather, gorse and bracken cloak the slowly-weathering volcanic hillsides, with the soil now gathered into the steep valleys where lush fields now exist. It is the continually changing pattern of rock and field that makes this area unique and gives it the nickname of Little Switzerland, a feeling enhanced by the lakes gathered in the old slate quarries.

Although the south-west is rather flat and visually unassuming, it contains much of historical interest. As you progress towards Market Harborough the land rises and falls, giving a more pleasing aspect to the eye. By contrast the north-east has dramatic views from the marlstone ridges around Belvoir over the low-lying plains of Nottinghamshire and Lincolnshire, with the countryside then gradually dipping down to Melton and the Wreake Valley.

In the south-east is Rutland, once England's smallest county and hopefully soon to be so again. The locals still consider themselves to be separate from Leicestershire and are fiercely independent. Their recent

Rutland passport is an indication of their feelings in this matter, and who can blame them? It is a most beautiful county, housing some of the most attractive villages in the country within its folds and hills. It is an ideal place for a holiday and well worth a week of anyone's time.

Hunting

"That Sire of the Chase – our crack Nimrod, old Meynell
Once said to a famed brother Sportsman of Quorn,
That "the fame and the fun of a Les'tershire kennel
Would cease – when the sun ceased to gladden the morn"
He's gone, but each year proves how true his prediction;
Unmarred is our sport – undiminished our fame,
He's gone, and this day shows his words were no fiction,
For "Hunting and Les'tershire" still mean the same."

Meltonian song, 1831.

Whether pro- or anti-hunting, what cannot be denied is the great impact that it has on the county. The field and hedge patterns have been retained in some areas largely because of the hunt, and many coverts were planted to give breeding territory for fox and fowl. The landscape of the east is particularly suited to the chase, as it is seldom waterlogged, has much grassland, wide fields and stout hedges. Here hunts the Cottesmore, based in Rutland, one of whose early Masters was Tom Noel of Exton, who wrote the first book on foxhunting in 1732.

Leicestershire has five hunts, the four "Shire" packs of Belvoir, Cottesmore, Fernie and Quorn, and the "Provincial" Atherstone. The season lasts from 1st September to the last Saturday in March, and attracts riders from all over the world. Should you wish to see the hunt then consult a local paper as to the time and place of the meet, Boxing Day is especially popular with its 11 a.m. starts from traditional venues.

Hugo Meynell, referred to in the above poem, is considered to be the founder of modern foxhunting with his systematic methods of hound breeding at Quorn. More recent enthusiasts include the Prince of Wales, who may often be found in the area along with assorted aristocrats and nouveau-riches. It does however attract a wide following from all walks of life and is more than just a social event for the wealthy.

People

Throughout the book you will find details of the famous and not so famous men and women associated with the places of the walks. There are many more characters whose paths we do not directly cross, but who have added to the shaping of the county.

Perhaps since this is a guidebook we should start with Thomas Cook, who organised the first commercial excursion in 1841 by rail from Leicester to a temperance meeting in Loughborough. 570 people paid the equivalent of 5 pence each for the trip. Soon the business expanded and in 1851 some 165,000 people made visits to London by train to see the Great Exhibition. His outings to the Paris Exhibition in 1855 were the start of the world-wide travel company that carries his name today.

Fenny Drayton was the birthplace of George Fox, founder of the Quakers. Another religious leader was Hugh Latimer, born in 1485 at Thurcaston, whose Protestant views saw him burnt at the stake with fellow Bishop Ridley. His final words, "Be of good comfort Master Ridley, and play the man, we shall this day light such a candle, by God's grace, in England as I trust shall never be put out", will be familiar to many people.

In Newarke Houses Museum, Leicester, can be found the chair and clothes of Daniel Lambert, reputedly the largest Englishman ever. Although a teetotaller and of modest appetite, he grew to weigh 52 stone 11 pounds at his death. He was a jailer at Bridewell Prison until it closed in 1805, after which he became an exhibit in London charging a shilling a head for those who wished to see him. He died whilst visiting Stamford in 1809, and the wall of the pub in which he was staying had to be demolished to allow the corpse to be removed.

Other unusual people were Joseph Merrick, the elephant man, and Jeffrey Hudson, a dwarf born in Oakham in 1619. Hudson was a favourite of the Duke of Buckingham, who once served him in a cold pie at Burley-on-the-Hill to Charles I. The Queen was much taken with

Hudson and he accompanied her on several trips abroad. He was still only 18 inches tall at the age of 30, but grew to be 45 inches tall in later life. He was captured by pirates, fought for the Dutch Army, killed a man in a duel, was imprisoned for alleged involvement in a Popish plot and was even a government spy before his death aged 63.

More recently Leicestershire has been the birthplace of Sir Richard and David Attenborough, whilst older readers will recall Lady Isobel Barnett who lived and died in the White House at Cossington. And Desert Orchid comes from Ab Kettleby.

Other Walks in Leicestershire and Rutland

In addition to the network of footpaths and bridleways, many excellently marked with the ubiquitous yellow posts and arrows by the thoughtful County Council, there are three official walks in the shire.

The Leicestershire Round is a 100 mile circular route, linking many interesting sites as it proceeds at a distance of between 5 and 15 miles from the centre of Leicester. Three booklets describing the route can be purchased from libraries and tourist information offices, and it is marked on the current series of Landranger maps. We will pass its distinctive markers on ten of our walks.

The Viking Way goes 120 miles from the Humber Bridge to its terminus in Oakham. The section in Leicestershire is about 24 miles long, described in a small leaflet from the usual sources, and it features in two of our north-eastern walks.

Finally the Jubilee Way, a more modest 15.5 miles long, was opened in 1977 to mark the Queen's Silver Jubilee. It links Melton Mowbray and Belvoir, is met in two of our walks and again has a small booklet associated with it.

1. HIGH CROSS

Route: High Cross – Frolesworth – Claybrooke Parva – High Cross

Distance: 8 miles, 13 kilometres. Old Roman road, some indistinct paths.

Map: O.S. Landranger 140 (Leicester and Coventry)

Start: High Cross bus stop on A5, by the junction of Fosse Way and the A5. Grid reference SP 473887.

Access: High Cross is 5 miles south-east of Hinckley on the A5. Hourly Avisdors X60 Hinckley to Lutterworth, Monday to Saturday. Car owners may prefer to park in one of the villages as High Cross is somewhat exposed.

Plough and Harrow, Frolesworth (0455 209347)

This friendly and comfortable pub is very much a local. It was built in the late 17th century, but much added to, and it used to be a favourite stopping off point for farmers after Westhorpe cattle market during the time that there was an all day licence. The tiled public used to be a butcher's shop , but now has a bar billiards table and old photographs of the Plough above the bar.

The lounge is also welcoming and comfortable, with an organist and sing-song at weekends, and there are both a garden and tables to the rear. The car park used to house the village school, whilst to the rear of the public house was a slaughterhouse. Bass, Worthington and an excellent Brew XI are available by handpump, and a range of meals and cobs can be purchased.

Open: Monday to Friday, 12 noon – 2 pm, (12 noon – 1 pm in winter) and 5 pm – 11 pm; Saturday, 12 – 11; Sunday, 12 – 3, 7 – 10.30

Food: Monday – Friday, 12 – 2; Saturday, 12 – 10.30; Sunday, 12 – 2.30.

High Cross

Only a hotel and a decaying monument mark the site of what was the Roman settlement of Venonae at the centre of their England. Here the 200-mile-long Fosse Way, from Bath to Lincoln, intersected Watling Street. The monument was erected in 1712 at the site where a wooden cross had stood for centuries, but after its disastrous encounter with lightning in 1791 the monument was relocated at its present position by the edge of the hotel car park. It is covered in 18th century graffiti, and carries a weathered inscription about a Roman commander, Claudius, who was buried nearby.

The Walk

1. Go to the hotel car park, and after viewing the monument pass through to the minor road behind it. Turn right past the hotel, itself an interesting building, until you encounter the Fosse Way information board to your left. Although rather badly faded and designed in a curious mix of colours, the board is full of information about the Roman road. It was originally 84 feet wide, with ditches at the side, the central area being raised to carry an 18 foot wide crushed stone carriageway.

   Turn left through the gate by the Leicestershire Round (L.R.) sign, following the obvious path down the side of the field. Here the ditches are visible, and it is possible to imagine what the road must have looked like. Pass through seven kissing gates, until after about 2 kilometres the track becomes a metaled road. Continue straight ahead as the L.R. turns off to the left, passing a car park and picnic tables. 300 metres later a ruined asbestos garage on the right indicates the start of the footpath to Frolesworth.

2. Turn right after the garage in the direction indicated by the sign, crossing the field by the clear path to a stile. The marked path goes straight across the next field towards the church, but locals turn right along the hedgerow and left along the bottom of the field. At the next hedge turn left, then right 50 metres later over a concrete slab and stile. Follow the barbed wire fence, pass the open barn and go up the farm track to the road. Continue along the road, noting the L.R. sign to the right which we shall return to later.

   Go past the church and through the village, with the road bending right and left, until you encounter the Plough and Harrow by a junction.

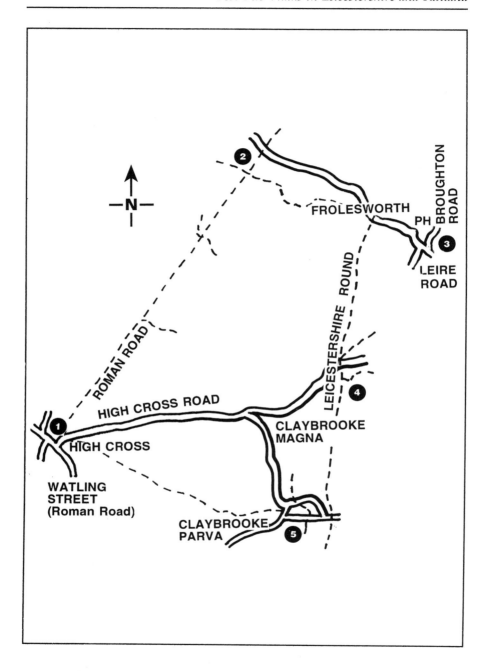

3. Opposite to the pub are some 18th century almshouses, endowed by a Chief Baron of the Exchequer in Scotland, John Smith, who is remembered by a plaque.

   Return through the village and turn left opposite White Cottage by the L.R. sign. Follow the track to the yellow waymarker, and head straight across the field in the direction of the farm to the next marker at the left-hand edge of the field.

   Cross the bridge and stiles, and go over the next field to an inconspicuous stile and L.R. sign. Traverse the stile and bridge, following the path near the right-hand hedge to the next concrete plank.

   Aim up the hill to a post on the skyline and the stile beyond. Go diagonally to the right, meeting a yellow post in the corner of the field. Cross the bridge and follow signs along the right-hand fence and stream. Climb a couple more stiles and then go left along the field edge to a road. Continue in the same direction along the path over the field, climbing a gate to the old mill pond.

4. The beautifully situated 18th century mill is on a much more ancient site, and has most of its machinery as well as an internal waterwheel intact. Turn left past the mill, then right over a new wooden footbridge with a L.R. sign to its right. Follow the path across the field, traversing the waste ground at the end to a small gate.

   Continue along the right-hand hedge and ditch through two fields to a gate. Go along the left-hand hedge to the next fence and down the tractor track to the farmyard beyond. Keep straight on to the main road, avoiding the right-hand farm road. Turn right, cross the road and head up the No Through Road past Claybrooke House.

5. After 100 metres turn right by the footpath sign into the church grounds. Go round the church, which will probably be locked although a key may be borrowed. It is well worth a visit because inside St Peter's is one of the finest chancels in any parish church in the country, c. 1340, framing the altar with its golden magnificence. There is also a touching wall memorial to Anna and Emma Dicey who both died in early adulthood.

   Leave the churchyard by the curved path to the main road, where you turn left. Continue past the school playground before turning left through a gate with the L.R. sign, by the side of the caretaker's house. Turn left up a concrete slab path around the back of the school, going right at the conifer hedge and past the small football pitch. Keep on with the hedge to your left through two fields to the next post by a barn. Cross the electric wire and farm track, from where the right of way heads slightly right across the field to a visible marker and stile, although locals usually keep to the left-hand field edge and come back along the field end to the yellow post.

Go over the footbridge and stile and follow the field boundary and stream to your left. Turn right at the stile and yellow marker and go along the path across the field. At the next post continue in the same direction to the marker by the sharp bend in the field, and follow the path to the stile ahead. Go over the footbridge and aim downhill to the left, passing to the right of two trees towards a single oak tree. Go up the triangular section, climbing the stile to the road.

Head left to the A5 and High Cross, which is to the right up the minor road.

2. PEATLING MAGNA

Route: Peatling Magna – Arnesby – Shearsby – Bruntingthorpe – Peatling Magna.

Distance: 6.2 miles, 10 kilometres. Excellent underfoot, mainly unspoilt pasture.

Map: O.S. Landranger 140 Leicester and Coventry

Start: Cock Inn, Peatling Magna. Grid reference SP 593926

Access: Peatling Magna is 7 miles south of Leicester. Infrequent United Counties bus number 60, Market Harborough to Leicester, gives limited access on Saturdays. Car parking is possible in the village.

Cock Inn (0533 478308)

This small pub boasts a comfortable beamed bar, with a fire and, on our Sunday lunchtime visit, table snacks. The right-hand side is used to serve an interesting variety of good quality food, and is particularly welcoming for a lazy Sunday lunch. The amiable landlord ensures a friendly and welcoming atmosphere in which to drink the John Smith and Courage Director's Bitters. The building is about 200 years old, and there are a few outside tables in the car park opposite. Please note that the pub does not open during weekday lunchtimes.

Open: Monday – Friday, 5.30 – 11; Saturday, 12 – 2.30, 6 – 11 Sunday, 12 – 3, 7 – 10.30

Food: Each day 7 – 9.15, plus Sunday, 12 – 2.30. Cobs available Saturday lunch.

Peatling Magna

Called Petlinge in the Domesday Book, this is one of the oldest settlements in Leicestershire, dating from the first century AD. Originally it covered a larger area, and the fields around, particularly in the vicinity of the church, show signs of the medieval house platforms. Most of the houses are 19th and 20th century, but many are built on older foundations and contain parts of earlier homes.

The well-sited 12th century church of All Saints contains monuments to the Jervis Family, one of which carries the phrase:
"as you are so were we; as we are so shall you be".

Tetty Jervis gained fame as the beloved wife of Samuel Johnson, whose dictionary was the first of its kind.

The Windmill, Arnesby

The Walk

1. At the road junction by the Cock Inn, take the gated road to Arnesby, Arnesby Lane. The church is passed to your right, and after passing through a gate across the road you will notice one of the sites of the medieval houses and some old earthworks in the field below All Saints.

   When the road bends sharply to the right we go left in the direction of the footpath signpost to Arnesby. There is no path on the ground, but as long as you keep going in the indicated direction then you will be all right. Aim initially for a post, resembling a sawn off telegraph pole, and follow the sheep track to the footbridge and iron handrail. Head through the gap in the fence opposite and continue with the hedge and ditch to your left. Go through a gap in the crossing hedge, maintaining your course to the next hedge. Carefully negotiate the fence and continue across the ridged field, evidence of its antiquity. When you go through a broken line of trees aim right towards the tall stile in the middle of the wire fence.

   This leads into a deer enclosure, containing the red deer hinds when we visited. Aim to the left, the next stile being directly in line with the restored windmill on the hillside. Continue along the same line to the next stile, from where you head slightly to the right of the mill for the stile. If the stags are in here take care not to disturb them by going too close.

   From here aim to the right of the open barn to the bridge and footpath sign. Keep along the top edge of the garden, whilst admiring the unexpected sights to the left. There you will find all manner of statues in front of the windmill, resplendent in its full sails from the 1970s refurbishment. A truly unique vista. Climb the stiles into and out of the driveway, turning right by the hedge to the road.

2. Arnesby dates from the 9th century and contains several timber framed houses. Sadly the old manor house has disappeared, leaving only its moat in the field below the church as a reminder. Cross the road and go down Mill Hill Road, taking the left fork up Church Lane. Pass by St Peter's Church and follow the road as it bends to the right. By Glebe Cottage go up the grassy lane indicated by the footpath sign, essentially continuing straight on.

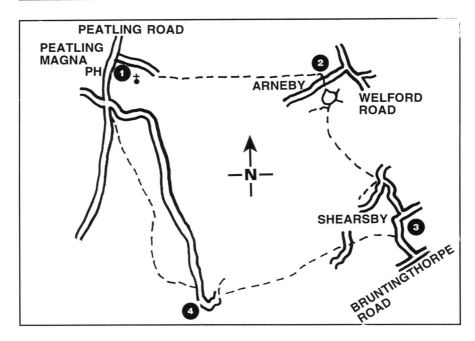

Mount the stile by the gate and go along the well worn path up the hill. Turn slightly left along the fence, cross two stiles and drop into what must have been an old lane judging by the flanking hedges. Climb the stile at the end, continue by the hedge and over the next stile. Follow the arrow as you keep by the left-hand hedge to the bottom of the field and across the railway sleeper bridge.

Continue to the next footbridge, go along the right-hand hedge and into a lane. Turn right along it to Shearsby.

3. This Saxon village undulates around the green, presenting a pleasant background for a stroll among its old buildings. The Chandlers Arms, formerly a candlemaker's cottage, dispenses Marston's Ales in its split-level interior and also serves an excellent Chicken Masala and other home-made dishes. To the south lies the Bath Hotel, a kilometre from the village, on the site of a salt spring that was once a spa but never really took off.

Enter the churchyard around the locked St Mary Magdalen, with its clusters of tombstones to the Reads, Seales and the splendidly named Hephzebah

Peberdy. Near to the holly tree by the main south entrance is the grave of William Weston:

"who unfortunately was catch'd in the Wind Mill and expired the 8th September 1782 in the 16th year of his age".

Leave by the path down to the main road, going across it and turning right by the telephone box to the Chandlers Arms. Continue up the road, going left at the end towards Bruntingthorpe. Turn right just before the speed derestriction signs by a Leicestershire Round (L.R.) sign. The path is obvious and zealously marked initially. After four stiles you come to a footbridge by the bottom of a hill. Follow the left-hand fence to the next stile, from where the marked path goes diagonally across the field. It may be polite to keep to the right-hand hedge if a crop is growing. Cross the next stile and go along the right-hand hedge towards the barn, and maintain the same direction to a stile.

Keep by the fence, turning left at the field end and ignoring the path to the right. Go into the lane through the gate, turning right past Salisbury House. At the main road you can turn left to the Plough, very much a local, serving Banks' Bitter, returning to here to continue to the right up the main road and past the turn off to the more upmarket and food orientated Joiners Arms.

4. Bruntingthorpe was home to the USAF as part of NATO, and the airfield to the south, now a testing ground, has the longest runway in Europe. As you walk through the village you pass White House Farm and its excellently restored 1717 Tithe Barn.

Continue to the edge of the village, turning left after Apple Tree House by the L.R. sign and stile. Go slightly right across the field to the yellow post and stile, where you follow the arrow to the next post. Head towards the marker in the middle of the clump of trees ahead, then follow the edge of the copse, ignoring the footbridge to the left.

Carry on with the ditch-cum-stream to your left, pass through a gate and cross a stile. A small brick pumping station is passed as you continue over a stile and follow the meandering, pretty stream. Climb a prominent stile and continue along the sheep track slightly left to the next stile. Eventually you cross a concrete bridge over the water and mount one final stile to the crossroads. Take the right-hand fork to Peatling Magna, enjoying the view to the church and no doubt the warmth of the Cock Inn.

3. FOXTON

Route: Foxton – Gumley – Foxton

Distance: 3.7 miles, 6 kilometres. Pleasant paths, quiet lanes and four pubs.

Map: O.S. Landranger 141 (Kettering and Corby)

Start: Foxton Post Office bus stop. Grid reference SP 903702

Access: Foxton is 3 miles north-west of Market Harborough. The Midland Fox X61/X62 Leicester to Market Harborough gives daily access, although returns may have to be made by walking the mile to the A6. Express services E143 offers an infrequent circular route from Market Harborough, Monday to Saturday. Parking is available in the village or on the car parks near Foxton Locks for a small fee, at SP 890692.

The Bell, Gumley (0533 792476)

A comfortable one room pub, about 300 years old, divided into lounge and public areas. The furnishings are comfortable and unobtrusive, but the delight for me is the small but enchanting rear garden. A wide variety of mature shrubs and plants give a distinctly old english cottage garden flavour, and it is a pleasure to sit there on a summer day. The beers available are currently Bass and Stones, but the new landlords may alter or extend the range as this is a freehouse. Dogs are not allowed inside because food is served.

Open: Monday – Saturday, 11 – 2.30, 6 – 11; Sunday, 12 – 3, 7 – 10.30

Food: 11 – 2, 6 – 10

Foxton

This quiet, attractive village would perhaps not be known at all were it not for the two important engineering achievements constructed on the

Grand Union Canal. The spectacular staircase of 10 locks, in two sets of 5, was built in 1808 and was considered to be a major engineering feat of the time. Boats took about 45 minutes to pass through, and so to avoid the congestion an inclined plane was built in 1900. This raised boats automatically to the top in only 12 minutes, and consisted of two tanks into which barges were floated, with a steam engine providing any necessary adjustment as the lowering of one raised the other through the required 75 feet. Unfortunately the scheme was uneconomic when canal traffic became less frequent, leading to its abandonment in 1911. The remains of the ramp can still be seen, and the museum at the locks displays a comprehensive model.

St Andrew's Church on the edge of the village probably marks the site of the first settlement in Foxton. It has been used by monks from about 850 AD, and the remains of a Saxon preaching cross which was discovered there can now be seen in the church opposite to the entrance. The workings of the old clock are also on display, as is a Norman font.

An informative leaflet "Walks around Foxton" is available from Leicestershire County Council at the usual Tourist Information outlets.

The Walk

1. From the Post Office turn left down Main Street, which curves around to the left. Go right up the driveway to the Shoulder of Mutton pub, going left across its beer garden to the yellow waymarker by the gate. Round the patch of nettles on the right to the stile by the arrow, heading slightly left across the next field past a large tree to an unmarked stile. Go right along the lane, turning left after 30 metres through the left-hand of two gates as indicated by the footpath sign.

   Head diagonally to the left through an open gateway and follow the edge of the stream to the lower stile by the blue gate. Follow the path over the stile and bridge, then through the cornfield with Gumley church in view ahead.

   Cross the bridge over the canal, then ignore the obvious path to Gumley by sticking to the right-hand hedge. After 100 metres a gate with a waymarker is negotiated, from where you aim left to the next marker between the two farm buildings.

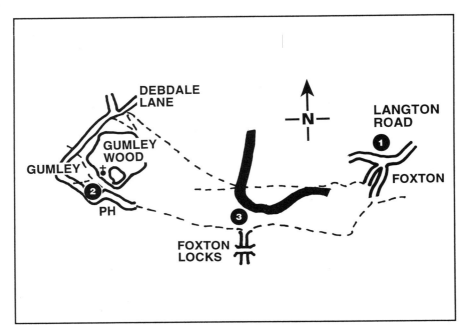

Go over the two stiles through the farmyard, cross the bridge and take the path across the field to the next post. From there aim diagonally left to a conspicuous white crossroads signpost where a gate leads on to the road. Turn left, passing the side of Gumley Wood and a house driveway before turning left at the Leicestershire Round sign. Through the gate aim past the glorious copper beeches to a gate at the right of the churchyard.

2. Enter St Helen's Church, which has a guidesheet about Gumley and the church itself. On leaving aim for the still working clock tower by the c. 1869 stables and exit on to the road.

Gumley, originally Gulmondeley or "Godmond's clearing in the forest", was probably an ancient site. It is known that the Mercian King Aethelbald held council here in 749. The hall was built in 1764 by Craddock, a friend of both Dr Johnson and Goldsmith, but was demolished in 1964. The lake and gardens, laid out by Capability Brown, remain.

Continue downhill from the Bell, taking the left-hand fork, and then 50 metres after the right-hand bend go left by the bridleway sign. Keep by the left-hand fence for a while before aiming at the gate in the end of the field. From there follow the track to the canal and Foxton Locks.

3. Have a good look around the locks, perhaps visiting the very reasonably priced museum first to get a better understanding of the inclined plane and the many pieces of canal engineering around the area. Quaffing a pint of Everard's outside the Bridge 61 is an alternative.

From there cross the brick bridge dated 1899 over the basin, passing the Foxton Boat services car park. The dirt and stone road passes several point-to-point fences, and just before the house if you look left over the hedge you will see the site of an old brickyard. This is actually a large depression, caused by the extraction of the clay for the bricks which have built much of Foxton and Gumley.

At the road go left, visiting St Andrew's church which dispenses peace and tranquillity, and then the Black Horse which dispenses the more earthly Marston's. Carry on down Main Street to the entrance to the Shoulder of Mutton and eventually back to the Post Office and bus stop.

Foxton Locks

4. WISTOW

Route: Wistow – Newton Harcourt – Kilby – Wistow

Distance: 5 miles, 8 kilometres. Well-marked paths.

Map: O.S. Landranger 140 (Leicester and Coventry)

Start: The Nooks car park, Wistow, grid reference SP 638959 or the Dog and Gun, Kilby, grid reference SP 621954.

Access: Wistow is 5 miles south east of Leicester. The car park is next to Wistow Hall garden centre but open to the public. Bus users will find it easier to use the Midland Fox 46 Leicester to Kibworth, alighting at the Dog and Gun in Kilby and starting the walk from there.

The Dog and Gun, Kilby (0533 402398)

The inn sign is worth a look, because above the painted board can be found an ironworked George and Dragon. This is testimony not to a former name of the pub, but to the fact that Mann's used to own the place. The old two room inn has been extended to make a comfortable bar and a lounge cum dining area, the bar containing a variety of artifacts including rugby programmes, old maps and cigarette cards.

Originally there were three buildings, a 17th century Tudor one flanked by two from the 18th century. The beers are Ruddles County and Best, Pedigree, Webster's and Bass all on handpump. Outside the large patio and garden can comfortably seat 100 people without it feeling crowded, and is also the place for barbecues on sunny days. One previous landlord used the back garden for breaking horses.

Open: Monday – Saturday, 11 – 2.30, 5.30 – 11; Sunday, 12 – 3, 7 – 10.30

Food: Daily, 12 – 2; Monday – Friday, 6 – 9; Saturday, 6 – 10; Sunday, 7 – 10

The Dog and Gun, Kilby

Wistow

There is little more to Wistow than the church and the hall, home of the Halford family and their descendants since 1603. The Jacobean hall is still privately owned, largely due to its having several flats for rent, and has housed many famous people over the years including Charles I on the eve of the Battle of Naseby. Indeed afterwards he fled here to change horses, and his saddle from the battle has been kept here ever since.

Sir Henry Halford was physician to four monarchs, from George III to Queen Victoria, and curiously was also the identifier of the body of Charles I when his lost coffin was rediscovered at Windsor. Allegedly he removed some of the neck bones, which bore the mark of the axe, and he would circulate these amongst guests at the dinner table. Eventually they were reunited with their owner after strong words from the Prince of Wales.

His son, also Sir Henry, was a fine marksman and shot for England many times. He was instrumental in the development of the .303 cartridge, and we will come across reminders of his prowess at two points on the walk.

The church of St Wistan's is built on the site of the grave of Wistan, Prince of Mercia, where after being murdered by his pagan uncle it is said that Wistan's hair grew from his tomb in the churchyard through the grass. Wistow is an abbreviation of Wistanstowe, the holy place of Wistan. Whilst the shell of the church is largely Norman, the interior is Georgian of stunning simplicity. Here may be found monuments to the two Sir Henry's and other Halfords, and a guide leaflet gives further details about Wistow and is well worth purchasing.

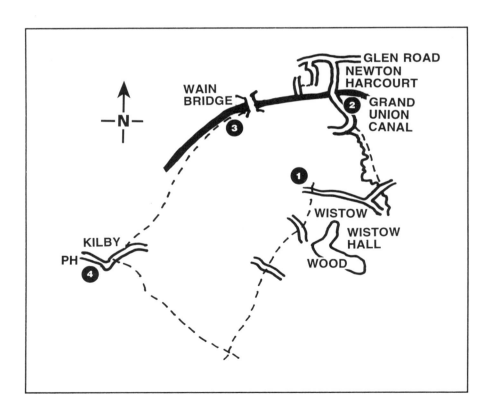

The Walk

1. Return to the main road from the car park and turn right, passing the garden centre and the grounds of the hall. At the end of the pavement cross over and go up the chipping covered drive to the church. Exit the churchyard by the path to the north, going through a gate at the end of the short grassy way. You are now on land open to the public and much used by locals for walking their dogs.

   Go right, crossing the footbridge and then turn left, aiming for the conspicuous yellow post in the right-hand corner of the field. A well-worn footpath should be met on the way. To the left beyond the meandering stream is the site of the deserted medieval village of Wistow, but little can be seen today.

   Cross the stile and continue over the field to the opposite gate which leads onto a minor road. Turn right, coming soon to the church of St Luke.

2. If you look at the weather vane on top, you will notice bullet holes in it. These were made by Sir Henry who saw from the Manor House opposite that it was not turning, and decided to give it some help. The Elizabethan manor house was renovated in the 19th century, but retains an impressive gateway. Sadly the presumed barn reconstruction to the right does not live up to the same standards, containing some rather ugly windows.

   The church was rebuilt from its Norman tower in 1834, and is usually locked. The churchyard however contains a most unusual gravestone, built in the shape of a miniature church, for Christopher Gardner who died in 1924, aged 8. Unfortunately it is showing signs of decay along with the rest of the graves, amongst which are several metal crosses marking what I take to be the resting places of paupers.

Continue down the lane, crossing the Grand Union Canal and the main Leicester to London railway before turning right up the main road into the village of Newton Harcourt. At the top turn left and then left again by a sign to a public telephone along a minor dead end street. Croft House Farm is passed before you turn right opposite the phone box along a tarmac footpath. Go through two kissing gates to a road, where you turn left and recross the railway. Cross a field, aiming to the left of the lock-keeper's cottage where you turn right along the towpath.

Pass under bridge 81 and turn immediately right up the narrow path to the road. Turn right, crossing the canal and then right again down some overgrown steps by a footpath sign. Cross a stile by a yellow marker and progress between wooden rails. As you pass a farm ignore the gate in front of you and take the pair of waymarked stiles just below to the left. Cross the small field, exiting by a stile in the bottom left onto the farm road which you follow.

3. After 150 metres a black and white metal sheet to your right looks suspiciously like a shooting target. It is, and yes it was Sir Henry who fired at it from some 2000 yards away at Wistow Hall. Fortunately it is not used today, so there is no need to duck.

Pass a yellow marker and mown roads which are part of a cross-country course on either side of our path. When a crossing hedge is met negotiate the stile and footbridge, from where you go straight on to the next marker and bridge. Aim for about a third of the way along the right-hand hedge where the next bridge is, then follow the arrow to a larger footbridge over the River Sence. Ahead lies a stile to the road, where you turn right and then bend right into Kilby village where the Dog and Gun awaits.

4. Return up the road, and as the turn to Fleckney is reached go through the gate by the footpath sign into a farmyard. Go to the left of the barn and climb the stile by the metal gate. Follow the direction of the arrow, passing the bend in the right-hand hedge to the next marker, by the corrugated iron shed. Pass through the gate, keeping by the left-hand hedge to a double stile. Cross the next field to a bridge and stile by a sapling, and maintain

your course to the next post. The same direction leads to a final stile, after which you go left along the bridlepath and not along the footpath ahead of you through the rape field.

After about half a mile Kilby Lodge and its majestic avenue of trees is met on your left. At the road go left over the cattle grid, from where Sir Henry's target is visible in front of you, then go right by the bridleway sign along the edge of Wistow Park to the car park.

5. HALLATON

Route: Hallaton – Glooston – Cranoe – Hallaton; (Optional addition of Goadby and Noseley)

Distance: 10 or 7 miles, 16 or 11 kilometres. Variable paths, quiet lanes.

Map: O.S. Landranger 141 (Kettering and Corby).

Start: The Green, by the Bewicke Arms. Grid reference SP 787965.

Access: Hallaton is 7 miles north-east of Market Harborough, set in the middle of country lanes. Fernie buses numbers 23 and 55 from Leicester to Market Harborough pass through on Tuesdays and Saturdays, and there is a once a month bus on Wednesday run by Deeward. Anyone not using a car will have to plan very carefully. Parking is available in the village.

Old Barn Inn, Glooston (085 884215)

This inn dates back to 1600, and although recently extended, retains an intimate atmosphere. Well-behaved children and dogs are welcome in the Cellar Bar, located to the rear of the pub. The gymnastics of the bar staff as they negotiate the steps between the upper dining area and the lower cellar can be entertaining, but pride of place goes to the range of real ales. Theakstones Best and X.B. are always available, alongside two guests from a range that includes Adnams, Batemans, Greene King, Fullers, Hook Norton and Morelands, and you may be pleased to notice that both keg beer and juke boxes are banned.

An extensive menu draws visitors from a wide area, consequently the attractive whitewashed cellar can be crowded on Sunday lunchtimes. With seats outside and a garden area, it is a fine place to be on a summer evening.

Open: Monday, 7 – 11 only. Tuesday – Saturday, 12 – 2, 7 – 11. Sunday, 12 – 2 only.

Food: 12 – 1.30, 7 – 9.30 when open.

Hallaton

A very picturesque village with thatched limestone and ironstone cottages, most of which have the dates on them. The Green contains a most unusually shaped village cross, its cylindrical base and conical top capped by a sphere, as well as a handsome war memorial. A plaque nearby gives details about the annual Easter Monday bottle-kicking and Hare Pie scrambling contests with nearby Medbourne, dating back to the 18th century.

The Butter Cross, Hallaton

The Hare Pie is distributed to onlookers by the rector in front of the church gate, with a portion being placed in a sack to be later scrambled for by the crowd, prior to the bottle-kicking.

The bottles are small casks, shaped like barrels. Two hold nine pints of beer each, whilst the third is an empty iron replica, painted blue, white and red. The basic aim is to get the bottle from Hare Pie Hill and back into your own parish, throwing it or kicking it to team mates. There are no fixed rules, and each game can last two hours. Three games are played, one for each bottle, with the victors displaying the trophies in their local.

The church of St Michael dates from Norman times and has several interesting features. In the porch is a Norman tympanum or door stone showing St Michael killing a dragon, whilst outside an obelisk is built into the wall as a commemoration to the Reverend George Fenwicke.

The village boasts three pubs. The Bewicke Arms serves home-made food and is 400 years old; the Olde Royal Oak in the High Street up from the green is a locals' pub; and the Fox Inn at the top of the village by the duck-pond is most unusual in having different pictures on its sign. One side shows a fox among spring bluebells, whilst the other side shows the same scene in autumn. All sell real ale; try them all, we did.

The Walk

Please note that as this walk was initially surveyed just after the autumn ploughing, many paths had disappeared. The good direction signs should ensure their restoration. If the route descriptions appear to be over-detailed for what may well be an obvious path, please bear with me.

1. From the Green head up Church Gate, the lane to the right of the church. Pass a school, and as the road turns right, go through a stile by a signpost indicating 2.5 miles to Goadby. Head across the middle of the field towards a single ash tree, crossing a stile and a stream by a prominent yellow post. These posts are our constant companions, the one 80 metres to the left will help us on the way back. Keep by the top of the field and go through the gate onto the road.

   To the left, the mounds of an old motte and bailey castle can be seen. Hallaton Castle was used by Ancient Britons, Roman coins have been found here and the Saxons also found its fortifications useful. Nothing remains of any stone building, but the ditches and grassy hillocks stand out clearly.

   Follow the road to the left, crossing the bridge by the ford, where the first decision of the day has to be made.

2. You can continue down this lane, Goadby Road, for the next two miles, or take the path by the fields which is of similar length. If going by road you will need to turn right at the end to Goadby, or left if taking the shorter walk to Glooston. It is a pleasant lane and in some ways preferable to the field path which is awkward in parts.

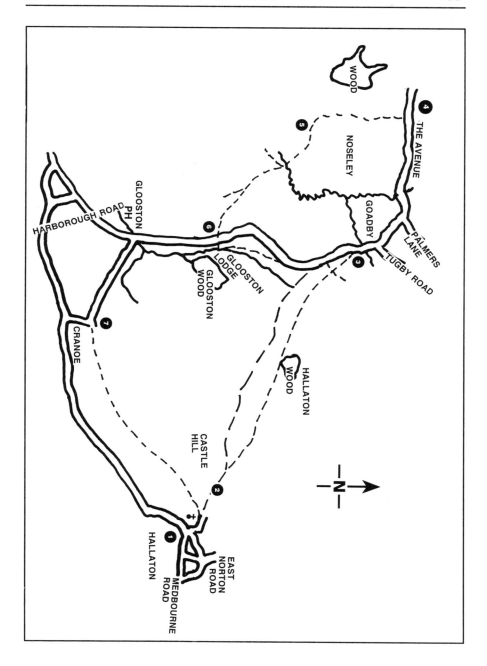

The field path starts up a bank to a stile, where a direction marker indicates the path around the right-hand edge of the field. In winter this is fine, but when rewalked in summer the field was a mass of rape which grew up to the edge. A path had been walked across the field, the right of way on the map, and this was in fact easier than trying to get around the field boundary, and led to the yellow post mentioned below. If going around the side, when a hedge is met keep going left along the field boundary until a yellow post is met near a lone tree. Follow the direction arrow diagonally across the field to a second marker in the top corner. Again this can be difficult in the rape season and not very pleasant.

Cross the stile and head right, crossing a small stream in the hedgerow by a footbridge hidden half-way along the right-hand hedge, into a large field. Head diagonally across, aiming initially for an isolated clump of small trees, from where a yellow post can be seen. Go to the post, cross the stile and proceed to the next marker. The arrow on top of the pole indicates that we go straight on to the next sign where a bridlepath crosses our way.

Climb the stile and go straight on with the hawthorn hedge to your right. Traverse the next stile and aim across the field to the post, underneath the house on the horizon. Cross the potato field, aiming at the white gate to the left of the house, Pine Tree Stud. Go through the gate and take the stile across the street into the horses' paddock. Aim for the yellow waymarker and stile in the middle of the fence opposite, then head down the middle of the next field to yet another stile, which leads you finally onto the road.

3. Here you may turn left and follow the road to Glooston, or you may turn right and walk the longer route through Noseley. The routes meet again at Glooston Lodge (6), a mile to the south of here.

   Go along the road to Goadby, take the first road left, signposted to Noseley, and then go straight through the village and down the hill. At the T-junction turn left, passing the wood and private road to Noseley Park. The gates are most impressive. Shortly afterwards turn left through a blue gate by a blue bridlepath arrow.

4. Follow the hedge and go through a second gate into a field whose undulations indicate the site of the deserted medieval village of Noseley. A third gate is negotiated near the lodge, leading onto a tractor path and dirt road. To the left the church and hall may be glimpsed through the trees,

historically the home of the Hesilrage family for generations. Go through the next gate, and as the road turns right, follow a blue arrow straight ahead to another gate. Here we turn left along the field's edge, and as we meet the woodland turn right with the field boundary.

After 100 metres we pass some young trees and conifers, then turn immediately left down a narrow unmarked path.

5. To your left is a pond, and a confirmatory waymarker appears to the right. Follow the obvious path ahead, coming out into a field between two wire netting edged enclosures. Continue straight ahead towards a solitary oak, and then go downhill to a gate by a stream. Cross the bridge and aim slightly right across the next field, to the right of the rightmost pylon partially visible on the skyline. As you reach the crest of the hill a prominent gate comes into view ahead, and we pass through it, keeping to the left-hand field boundary until a second gate is met near the electricity cables. Pass through the gate, head diagonally across the field to an isolated clump of trees and then follow the hollow down to an old iron gate. Keep the fence to your right and cross a second gate before emerging on the road by Glooston Lodge.

6. Turn right, and after a kilometre turn right at the crossroads to the Old Barn. Suitably refreshed, return to the crossroads and carry straight on towards Cranoe, the headland of the crows. In a further kilometre as the church is reached, the road turns sharply to the right, but we go left through a gate with two footpath signs.

7. Turn right, following the Leicestershire Round sign towards a telegraph pole, from where a yellow post and stile become visible ahead. Cross the stile and follow the field edge to another post. In the next field keep the hedge to your left, go through a gate and then another to the left of Othorpe House. Skirt the barn on its left, and pass through the next gate. To the right lies the deserted medieval village of Othorpe, although it is not too apparent on the ground.

Go through the gate, aiming slightly left along the path to another one of our yellow companions, cross the bridge and then continue along the path to a further marker. From here the route is straight ahead to the conspicuous gap and ubiquitous post, then follow the arrow slightly right to a small fenced pond. From there our route deviates to the left towards the grassy mounds of Castle Hill.

A double stile and arrow point the way to a waymarker, from where you aim slightly right to a footbridge at the bottom of the field. Avoid the obvious path right over another bridge, aiming instead for the corner of the field ahead. Cross a plank bridge and stile, aim across the field to the next post and then go by the cemetery wall until the gate is reached. Head down the lane past the church to The Green and refreshment.

6. LYDDINGTON

Route: Lyddington – Seaton – Bisbrooke – Lyddington

Distance: 6 miles, 9.5 kilometres. Fields and quiet lanes.

Map: O.S. Landranger 141 (Kettering and Corby).

Start: Bus shelter by Old White Hart, Lyddington. (Grid reference SP 875971)

Access: Lyddington is 2 miles south of Uppingham. The United Counties bus from Uppingham to Corby gives an infrequent weekday service. Other irregular buses to Corby and Leicester. On road parking is available in the village.

George and Dragon, Seaton (0572 87773)

The pub has recently reopened after sympathetic extension and alteration. It is known to have been a pub in 1833, and has since taken over what were the neighbouring greengrocer and butcher. To the left is a simple bar with a pool table, whilst on the right the fire-warmed lounge is simply and tastefully furnished. The date outside is 1879, but the lounge retains the structure of the old cottages from which it was converted. There is an inviting restaurant to the rear, which serves a wide variety of food. Theakstone's bitter, Younger's IPA and Bass are well kept and served, and the friendly aura of the pub is testimony to the landlords Chris and Janet Pearce.

Open: Monday – Saturday, 11 – 3, 5.30 – 11; Sunday, 12 – 3, 7 – 10.30

Food: Every day 12 – 2.30, 7 – 10 in bar or restaurant.

Lyddington

This Rutland village takes its name from *hylde tun*, meaning a settlement by a noisy stream. Nowadays the noisy stream is more likely to be that of tourists, heading for the two fine inns and the Bede House. The latter was built as a bishop's residence in the 15th century, but in 1602 Lord Burghley converted it into a hospital. The name comes from the bedesmen, people who were paid to pray for others, and the 16th century ceiling is particularly fine. It is now owned by English Heritage and open daily from 29 March to 30 September.

The village contains many ironstone houses, quarried nearby at Stoke Dry, the date stones of which enable you to study the changes in architecture during the 17th and 18th centuries.

The inns both serve excellent food and are justifiably popular. The Marquess of Exeter offers Ruddles, Bateman's and Theakstone's in a comfortable lounge bar, and it also does accommodation. The thatched roof contains a surprise on top. The Old White Hart serves Greene King ales, has several cosy bars and a floodlit petanque court available for hire.

The George and Dragon, Seaton

The Walk

1. From the bus shelter by the green, with its stump of a cross, head left towards the church, then turn left by the Bishop's watch tower, built into the corner of the Bede House's garden wall. Go through the gate and into the 14th century St Andrew's Church. Interesting features include the altar rails from 1635, allowing access on all four sides, and the earthenware jars embedded in the top of the side walls of the chancel in order to improve the acoustics. A booklet gives further details, and there are good explanations around the church.

   On leaving the church, turn right and go through the archway of the Bede House, following the gravel path left up Bluecoat Lane to the edge of the green. Turn right by the footpath sign and take the right-hand stile by a gate into a field. Keep to the left-hand edge of the field, noting the hollows of the old fish-ponds on the right, and at the top turn left over a muddy bridge into a narrow field.

   Cross the stile onto the old lane, turn right and take the right-hand stile next to the gate. Keep to the left of the field, where the newly planted trees will cover Prestley Hill next century, and cross a stile, keeping close to the left-hand side. To the right the spire of Seaton Church can be seen, which is our destination.

   As the hedge turns left, go right by a ditch, then turn left 25 metres later along a good path. When a tractor track is met turn right along it to Seaton Grange Farm. The three-quarter mile long Welland Viaduct can be seen away to the right straddling the boundary with Northants. Completed in 1882, it took 4 years to build, the 2000 labourers being housed in a temporary village called Cyprus. Continue along the track past the farm, turning right up the road to Seaton.

2. At the junction with Moles Lane, opposite Homestead (number 11), steps up the bank on the left-hand side lead to a stile. This should be noted as it will be our route on the way back. Continue through the village past the church and into the George and Dragon. After quenching your thirst return to All Hallows Church; the yew covered graveyard is most attractive and there is an impressive chest, said to have been used for collecting monies for the crusades of Richard the First, in the porch by the notable Norman doorway.

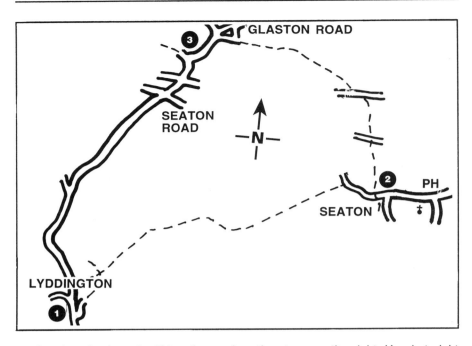

Continue back to the T-junction and up the steps on the right. Head straight across the field to the stile, turn right and after 20 metres, go left up the boundary strip between two fields. At the top, just over the brow of the hill, go left then right 35 metres later along another field boundary. An old corrugated barn is passed to your left as we go right then quickly left again. Head down to the stream with a close cropped hedge on your right, climbing the iron rails at the bottom onto a disused railway line, now a farm track.

Turn left up the track, and after 70 metres go right through a gate. Aim downhill by a tractor path to the junction of two streams, crossing the first near a conspicuous pile of stones. Walk with the second stream to your right, and at a bridge head off slightly uphill to your left in the direction of Bisbrooke church, whose spire looms over the horizon. Cross a stile to the right of a small aluminium gate onto a well worn path, which we follow to St John's Church. This modern church is pleasantly situated but of no great interest, so continue along the lane past it, turning left as the road is reached. Follow the road downhill to the Gate Inn.

This traditional pub serves Ruddles County but not meals, and has a cosy bar, neat lounge, and swings in the garden. The landlady and her dog Sam offer a warm welcome. At the road turn right towards the now missing railway bridge, and go straight on at the crossroads. Extensive views to the left enable you to see the route that you have walked, and add greatly to the enjoyment as you continue down the road into Lyddington and its hostelries.

7. MARKET BOSWORTH

Route: Market Bosworth – Sutton Cheney – Bosworth Battlefield – Market Bosworth.

Distance: 5 miles, 8 kilometres, plus optional 1.8 mile Battle Trail. Excellent paths, a real joy.

Map: O.S. Landranger 140 (Leicester and Coventry)

Start: The Market Square, Market Bosworth. Grid reference SK 405030

Access: Market Bosworth is 12 miles west of Leicester, off the A447. The Leicester City bus 153 gives frequent access, and the Stevenson 179 Hinckley to Coalville can also be used. Parking in the village is possible, but easier towards Bosworth Park.

Black Horse Inn, Market Bosworth (0455 290278)

Set on the Market Square, this is a splendid old low-ceilinged pub, serving Pedigree, Tetley's, John Smith's bitter and Addlestones cider. Parts of the inn are thought to be 16th century.

The lounge contains old photographs of the town and a small statue in the area leading to the restaurant. The latter occupies three former cottages, cleverly knocked through to retain the separate areas, whilst maintaining discreet divisions. The menu is both extensive and reasonably priced, with the snacks option to some main meals sufficient in themselves for lunch and probably the largest piece of cheesecake I've ever seen.

Open: Monday and Wednesday, 10 – 3, 6 – 11; Tuesday, Thursday and Friday, 11 – 2.30, 6 – 11; Saturday, 10.30 – 3, 6 – 11; Sunday, 11 – 3, 7 – 10.30

Food: Monday – Saturday, 12 – 2 (hot) and 2.30 (cold), 6 – 10; Sunday, 12 – 2, 7 – 10

Market Bosworth

Bosworth is forever linked to the battle in which Henry Tudor defeated Richard III, which is rather odd because it actually took place in Sutton Cheney. The story of the battle is well explained on the site which we will visit on the walk. The town itself retains much of its 19th century appearance, especially around the square, which has had a Wednesday market since 1285, and also has a cattle market on Monday mornings. Shields bearing the coats of arms of the participants in the fight adorn the houses, and the hanging baskets won for Bosworth the 'Britain in Bloom' competition in 1988. There is also a station on the private steam line from Shackerstone to Shenton, which can be used to return from the walk, and the Ashby Canal is near-by.

The church of St Peter contains interesting monuments to the Dixie family, former owners of the Hall, and an ancient font. A leaflet describes the main features. Outside and to the east of the south porch can be found the grave of Robert Pull, partially overgrown near to the foot of the yew trees. He was a quack doctor, highly regarded by the locals, but local legend suggests that his "sudden departure" at the age of 60 was due to his being buried alive.

The Hall is now a hotel, whose excellent value winter breaks are worth checking out, and although much altered both in the 19th century and more recently, presents a grand facade. Opposite to it is Bosworth Country Park, which possesses picnic tables and fishing among its amenities.

The Walk

1. From the square turn right up Main Street and right again past the Dixies Arms. Continue along the road as it turns right in front of Ye Olde Red Lion, going left 100 metres later after number 31 down a tarmac drive to the church of St Peter.

   Return to the road, going left, and as the expanse of Bosworth Park is seen ahead, cross the road at the junction. Follow the left-hand side of the fence past the Inn on the Park, continuing to Bow Pool. Skirt the right-hand side of the pond, and at the end turn right along a grassy path through the trees. At

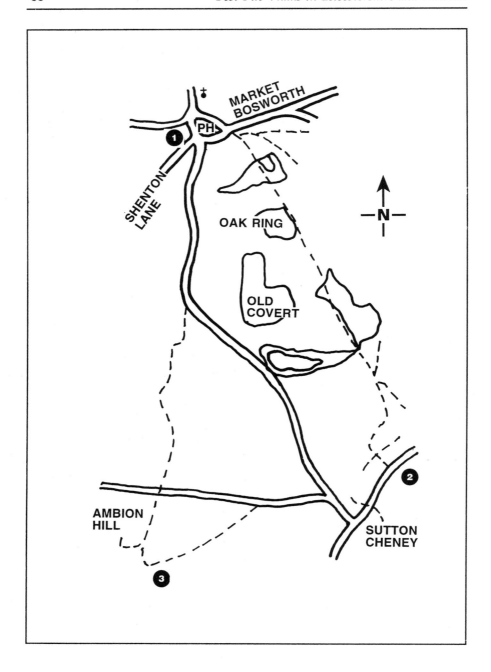

the end across a dirt path is a yellow waymarker by a handgate – don't use the stile some 100 metres to the left of here.

Go carefully through the giant hogweed patch and make your way along a grassy ride, originally a road to the Hall, and known as Lady Agnes' drive. To the left in a field stands a cemented cairn, a monument to a horse, whilst on your left the wood of Oak Ring is met. At the end of the wood look right where the top of a statue of Hercules, formerly the top of an 18th century monument, may just be seen over the horizon. This will be better seen on the way back.

Pass Looking Glass pond, cross two stiles by the side of the mock Tudor Woodhouse Farm, built as a Keeper's lodge, and continue down to the bridge. On the right an old sluice gate and dam can be seen, as you continue along the track past the Leicestershire Round sign with the hedge on your right. As the hedge turns right continue straight on up a path to a yellow post on the skyline, leaving the farm track. There turn sharp right along the hedge, and at its end turn left, ignoring the arrows on the post and taking the path to your left which aims straight for the rear of a house. This turns out to be the Royal Court pub, the footpath going through its garden and past the conservatory to the road. There are a variety of good ales and a tempting menu, so perhaps a pause is called for.

2. At the road turn right, passing the impressive Hall Farm on the way to the Hercules, a 16th century coaching inn which served several real ales including Stonehenge Bitter and Speckled Hen during our visit. Whether the pub was named after the statue or what relationship there is between them is not known to me. Perhaps you could find out for homework. On leaving continue down the road, taking the path right to St James's Church.

The "Battlefield Church" is where Richard III is said to have received mass on the eve of Bosworth Field, and inside a wall plaque from the Society of Richard III marks this. Another memorial on the south wall is to Thomas Simpson, a noted amateur mathematician, who started out as an astrologer and oracle before gaining immortality as the inventor of Simpson's Rule, so familiar to mathematics students. A guide inside to the 13th century church can be found.

To the right of the church is a row of Almshouses, founded in 1612 by Sir William Roberts. The top half was rebuilt in 1811, and they have now been converted into a bar/restaurant.

Leave the churchyard to the west, through a handgate, turning right at the road and then left at the junction towards Shenton. In front of you is Ambion Hill, the site of the battle, and you may now see the pennants flying over the positions occupied by the various troops. Go left into the car park and take the path through the handgate behind the large sign on the right. Continue on to the Battlefield Centre, which houses an interesting exhibition of models of the armies and an explanation of life in the late 15th century.

3. The well stocked gift shop and information centre is most helpful, but if you have the time the Battle Trail walk, which is always open, is the highlight of the area with its clear explanations. The start is by the car park next to the centre. Special events include jousting and the re-enactment of the battle, and the centre is open from 1st July to 31st August.

Leave the centre by the road from the main car park, heading towards Market Bosworth on the horizon. At the main road go straight across and over a footbridge and stile to join a path to a gap in the hedge slightly to the right. Continue along the path as it goes diagonally left, passing close by the corner of the opposite hedge where you head a touch right to a yellow post. From there the next post and plank bridge are apparent, and you travel along with the hedge to your right. At the corner head across to another marker, cross a stile and eventually a bridge onto the road. Turn left and walk the kilometre or so to the town. On your right the statue of Hercules glimpsed before is now more obvious on the skyline.

8. SHACKERSTONE

Route: Shackerstone – Congerstone – Little Twycross – Shackerstone

Distance: 5.5 miles, 9 kilometres. Undefined paths, quiet road and canal side.

Map: O.S. Landranger 140 (Leicester and Coventry).

Start: Turn Bridge (number 52) over the Ashby Canal, Shackerstone. Grid reference SK 367067.

Access: Shackerstone is 4 miles north-west of Market Bosworth. Access by bus is very difficult, and you will either need a car or to use the Battlefield Line railway from Shenton or Market Bosworth. This runs on Sundays and Bank Holidays, March to October, and Saturdays in July and August. Leaflets can be had locally or contact the Shackerstone Railway Society on 0827 880 754 for further details. Car parking is possible near to the station or in the village.

Rising Sun, Shackerstone (0827 880215)

A friendly and comfortable pub that prides itself on an extensive and reasonably priced menu, served in the interesting restaurant, which used to be a barn, then a skittles alley. The brickwork is most irregular, being constructed in Ibstock Blobs. According to local legend, the variety of brick sizes is due to the brickmakers protesting at their working conditions by producing enormous bricks rather than going on strike. However it may possibly have something to do with the brick taxation laws, as tax was per brick and not by size.

The lounge bar is wood panelled, with a public containing a pool table at the rear. Pedigree and a guest beer, Fuller's when we last visited, are the well-kept beers, and if you are lucky there are nibbles in the form of black pudding and cheese at the bar on Sunday lunchtimes. There is a ghost which has been seen twice, once in the cellar and once in one of the bedrooms, dressed like a prisoner of war. Families are most welcome, and there are seats and a garden to the side.

Open: Monday – Saturday, 12 – 2.30, 6.30 – 11; Sunday, 12 – 2.30, 6.30 – 10.30

Food: Every day 12 – 2, 7 – 10

The Rising Sun

Shackerstone

This is an old village, dating back to Saxon times. Beads of amber and glass from that period have been found, but the main interest lies in two more recent developments; the canal and the railway.

The Ashby Canal was originally intended to go as far as the River Trent, but the problems involved saw it remain as a 30.5 mile lockless waterway, following the 300 foot contour. It was mainly used to carry coal from the Moira end, but subsidence in that area led to the closure of the northern 8 miles.

Nearby is the station for the Battlefield Line, a 5 mile standard gauge steam railway running from Shackerstone to Shenton, near to Bosworth Field. There is an interesting museum of "Railwayana" at the station, much of it from local lines, and both tea and gift shops are included.

The Walk

1. At Turn Bridge the towpath changes sides. Go down the path to the left of the bridge signposted to Congerstone, and proceed under the bridge and down the towpath. Opposite glimpses of the station and perhaps a train can be had, as you continue past Bates Wharf and Bates Bridge before turning off to the right just under Terrace Bridge (number 49). Climb two stiles to the road. turning left and then left again at the main road to the green.

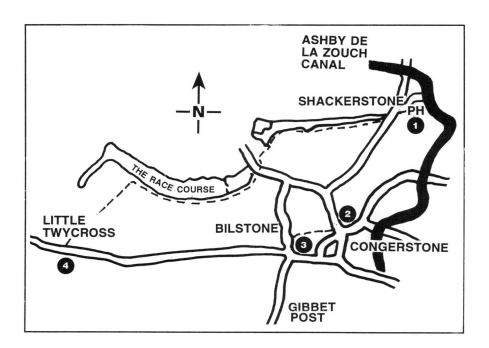

2. Turn right along the road towards Shackerstone, and then quickly left by the footpath sign to skirt the side of St Mary's Church. The church was largely restored in 1834 and is of interest architecturally. It contains box pews, an unusually wide chancel, cast iron tracery and a fireplace next to the squire's pew. It may well be locked however, but use the side gate to check.

    Continue past the church to a gate, and head across the field by an intermittent line of posts to a handgate and footbridge. Keep going to a stile or gap in the fence in front of the old mill, partially in need of attention. Follow the track to the road where you turn left towards a triangular green.

    At this point an 800 metre diversion can be made by continuing up the road, ignoring the right-hand turning to Twycross and then the left-hand turning to Congerstone and Market Bosworth, eventually coming to a gibbet post. This was erected in 1801 for the body of John Massey after his execution at Birstall. Massey, also known as Topsey Turvey, was hanged for the murder of his wife, and the gibbet is one of the few surviving in England. Return to the green afterwards.

3. Take the road towards Twycross, and follow it for 2 kilometres, passing the driveway to Gopsall House before turning right by a footpath sign just before a barn on the left.

4. The route from here is indistinct on the ground, and not waymarked. It appears in parts to be deliberately neglected, but the more that it is walked the better it will become, and the scenery is very pleasant. Head across the field in the direction of the sign to climb the fence near the right-hand corner. Aim towards the farm of Gopsall House, again climbing a fence, then head towards the barns and a stag-headed oak. Negotiate the cattle wire and go through the gateway to the right of the oak.

    Follow the cart-track and climb the fence in the diagonal right-hand corner. Turn right along the field edge through an open gateway, then left along the hedge at the field side. At the bottom turn right for 30 metres, then left across a grassy bridge by an unused telegraph pole. Go to the wood edge and turn right along it. Pass through two hedges and a butchered hedgerow until a section of woodland appears in front of you. There turn left into the wood, called the Race Course on maps.

    The right of way is totally overgrown and impossible to trace. Instead go into the wood for 20 metres to a grassy ride. This is well used by horses and can be muddy, but the surrounding trees house sufficient wildlife to make the journey a pleasant one. Continue along the 5 metre wide track and climb the fence at the end. Again the footpath has disappeared, so the least damaging route is to go left along the wood side, and turn right along the barbed-wire fence. If you are lucky then you may hear quail in the field and possibly glimpse one of these small partridges. At the end the easiest way over the wire is to go right, climb the gate and then return down the road.

5. You are now well inside Gopsall Park, begun in 1747 by Charles Jennens, a spectacularly rich man who included Handel amongst his friends. It is believed that he wrote part of the Messiah here, as well as the music to the hymn "Rejoice the Lord is King" whose tune is called Gopsall. Sadly the house was demolished in 1951 due to its neglect and disrepair by the Crown, who purchased it after the Second World War when it had been a garrison for troops. The estate comprised over 1000 acres, but many cottages have been sold off, with the Crown retaining the farm. The relationship between the Crown and Leicestershire County Council is not as healthy as it might be, and this has not helped the footpath route.

Again the marked footpath is unusable, although some sort of compromise has been made over the right of way. Turn right off the farm road through the gate, with the barbed wire and new trees to your right. At the wood climb the fence to your right and cross a new plank bridge. Go left along the edge of the wood, cross another bridge and then go through a gate onto a dirt road. Turn left then go right over a bridge to a handgate. Pass through another gate and continue along the side of the wood.

This is yet another diversion from the right of way through the woodland, but the bridges are a compromise to keep walkers out of the wood which has private shooting rights. Cross yet another bridge, this time by a footpath sign, keeping to the field edge. At the end a garden blocks the way, so turn right for 30 metres, climb the barbed-wire fence by the tree stump and follow the path to the road. Turn left, where you will soon pass a footpath sign on your right. This officially points the way to the path that we have come down, but instead is totally useless. It leads down the house drive either to a locked gate or the garden fence. The gentleman who lives there suggests that the path probably goes through his bathroom, but iunless the concerned parties reach some agreement then it may as well not be there.

After 200 metres turn right by the sign to the Rising Sun, down Church Road. From the pub a continuation and right turn lead to the canal bridge and station.

9. BILLESDON

Route: Billesdon Circular

Distance: 6.3 miles, 10 kilometres. Good paths and quiet lanes.

Map: O.S. Landranger 141 (Kettering and Corby)

Start: Market Place, Billesdon. Grid reference SK 028719

Access: Billesdon is nine miles east of Leicester just off the A47. The Express Services X47, Leicester to Uppingham and Peterborough gives the most frequent access, but other buses also pass through. Parking is easy near the Market Place.

The Queen's Head, Billesdon (053755 352)

Serving Everard's Beacon, Tiger, Old Original and Adnams Bitter, this is one of the oldest buildings in the village. It has been a pub for over 200 years and was a private dwelling before that. There is a separate public bar, as smart as many lounges, and a comfortable oak-beamed lounge that has been extended to include a conservatory. A wide range of foods is available, and there is an upstairs restaurant. There are a few outside tables, and a disabled persons' toilet across from the lounge.

Open: Monday – Saturday, 11 – 2.30, 5 – 11; Sunday, 12 – 3, 7 – 10.30

Food: Every lunchtime 12 – 2; Tuesday – Saturday, 7 – 9.30

Billesdon

The name means Bills Hill, and it was originally applied to the nearby Billesdon Coplow, where Saxon brooches have been found. A detailed town trail leaflet is published by Harborough District Council and can be obtained at Tourist Information Offices. Many of the oldest buildings are gathered around the church, and old mud walls may still be seen. The Old School of 1650 has an explanatory plaque on the wall, the early 17th century "Old Vicarage" contains typical stone mullions and transoms, whilst my personal favourite is the 17th century Tithe Cottage. This is a conversion from the original barn in which the vicar would store his tithe or tenth of the crops and stock produced by the inhabitants.

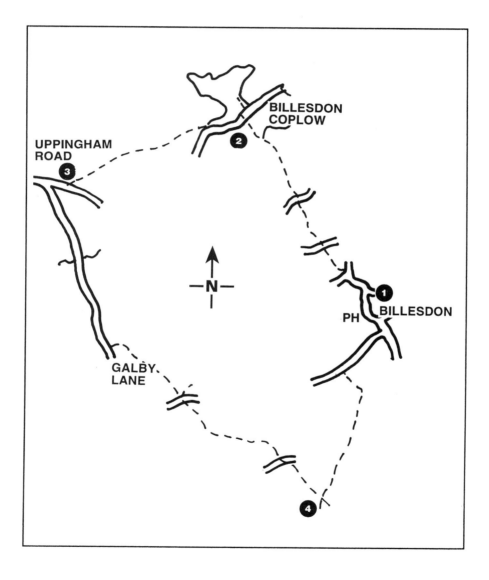

The Walk

1. Head from the Market Place along the main road towards Leicester, passing the White Hart and turning right up Coplow Lane by the signpost to Keyham. After 50 metres turn left by a footpath sign up a narrow gap between two tall hedges. Turn right along the hedge and when it turns right head straight across to a stile.

    Carefully cross the bypass and its attendant stiles, keeping to the top of the hill to the next stile hidden in a hedgerow. Go across to a dwarf stile and take the faint path across the field, aiming for the hill in front. Go over and under the fences, walking parallel to the old strip farming mounds to a footbridge. Maintain your direction, duck under a barbed wire strand and then climb a fence. This brings you onto a path crossing a grassy bridge over a ditch before going right to a gap in the hedge.

    Cross a nettle-festooned ditch and head across the field towards the telegraph pole in the corner. Just to its left is a footbridge which you cross. Go over the fence opposite, unhooking the electric cable from the shed and replacing it, then follow the right-hand hedge to the farm. Pass through two gates and then go up the farm road.

    The walk is a lot nicer than the above description would indicate!

2. To the right is Billesdon Coplow, meaning summit and presumably burial mound, a high wooded hill which is the crossing point of several primitive trackways. It was, in 1829, the finishing point for the first cross-country horse race in England, with Captain Beecher one of the competitors. He became famous in association with the brook at Aintree. The impressive building is Coplow House, built in 1790, which could be seen from over 7 miles away when originally constructed before the trees matured. It was extended and refurbished in 1842 to its present Georgian style.

    Continue through the griffin topped gates, turning left at the main road. Just before the left-hand bend a wobbly signpost to the right indicates the way over a rickety fence. Go left along the tractor prints, where a kindly and sensible farmer has reinstated the footpath after ploughing. A defunct hedge is crossed as the path heads towards a telegraph pole 100 metres away to the left of the prominent silos.

The track towards the silos is joined for a short while until we re-meet the helpful tractor guidelines and pass the telegraph pole to cross a footbridge. Go right along the hedge, then left up the field edge or along tractor marks to the signpost in the corner of the field.

3. Turn right up the roadside pavement, soon crossing over to head down the road to Frisby and Gaulby, Gaulby Lane.

Continue for about a mile down this pleasant open lane before turning left by a footpath sign along a farm road. Keep with it as it goes left, eventually arriving at a road. Cross over and go down the driveway past Frisby House Farm, and when it degenerates into a muddy track, accompany it left past a large green tank atop a breeze-block hut. The track is followed for a kilometre through several twists and turns, becoming less distinct as it changes to the right-hand side of the hedgerow.

4. After a small horse-trough is passed turn left along a wide bridleway through two large rape fields. Pass through a small gate and follow close by the right-hand hedge, turning left through a waymarked gate shortly before the field end. This is taken to the road, where a right turn leads to the village. Turn left at the Church Street junction, passing the Old Vicarage with its interesting bay windows, the Old School, the church of St John and the Quadrant on your way to the Queen's Head. From there continue up the street to the Market Place and the start.

10. BELTON-IN-RUTLAND

Route: Belton – Leigh Lodge – Withcote Hall – Launde Abbey – Belton.

Distance: 10 miles, 16 kilometres or 7 mile option. Quiet lanes and bridlepaths through unspoilt and open countryside. One of the best walks in the book.

Map: O.S. Landranger 141 (Kettering and Corby)

Start: Sun Inn, Belton. Grid reference SK 817013

Access: Belton lies just off the A47, 4 miles west of Uppingham. By bus, the infrequent Express Service X47 Leicester – Uppingham – Peterborough stops near to the Sun Inn. Car parking is possible in the village.

Sun Inn. (057 286227)

This 16th century building has been a pub for over 250 years, although it was originally a wheelwright's shop. Inside there are two linked areas, one with a fireplace, in which to drink the excellent Banks's mild and bitter. Hot meals, including home-made and vegetarian dishes, are available, and the Sun also has a games room and beer garden. The pub has been run by the same family for 24 years, Bernie and Trish Crouch being the second generation licensees.

Open: Monday – Saturday, 12 – 2.30, 6 – 11.00; Sunday, 12 – 2.30, 7 – 10.30

Food: Summer, Tuesday – Sunday, 12 – 1.45, 7 – 9.45; Winter, Wednesday – Saturday, 12 – 1.45, 7 – 9.45

Belton-in-Rutland

Not to be confused with Belton in Leicestershire, this ironstone village has a cluster of interesting and attractive houses to the north end around the church of St Peter. The latter is usually locked, but the 15th century tower, bristling with gargoyles, is most entertaining.

There are fine rows of cottages with stone mullioned windows, Hillcrest being a particularly fine building. Also worth tracking down are the 17th century Old Hall, Godfrey's House and the 18th century Westbourne House. The war memorial has an older base, where tradition maintains that Charles I rested on his flight from the Battle of Naseby.

The Walk

1. Turn right from the Sun along Main Street, then go left up Chapel Street, with Hillcrest on the left. At the signpost take the right-hand fork towards Lambley Lodge. When the road turns to the left, continue straight up the unmarked but well-ridden and probably muddy bridlepath to the right of the overgrown hedgerow.

   When you come to a farm road turn left towards the barns, pausing to admire the view in front of you. This area contains no metaled roads and is probably the largest such area in Leicestershire and Rutland, but the intensive farming makes certain that it is not a wilderness. Just before the barns, turn right at a bridlepath sign down the excellent track, and cross the embryonic River Chatham to Leigh Lodge. The latter seems to be in a process of renovation.

2. Pass the lodge, and turn left along its northern side down a rubble road that soon becomes a muddy track. To the left the old fish ponds are now full of water, as we continue along the muddy tractor path straight across the field to a gap in the hedge. The path turns a little to the right, crosses a small stream in an attractive valley and goes slightly left over the next field. When you pass through a hedgerow the way is diverted to the right around the field edge which we follow with the hedge to our right.

   When you come across a post with three bridlepath and one footpath signs continue straight on, but this time with the hedge to your left, for 350 metres.

3. A signpost is met, where it is possible to take a shortcut and knock three miles off the walk by taking the left-hand path to Launde Abbey, point 6 on

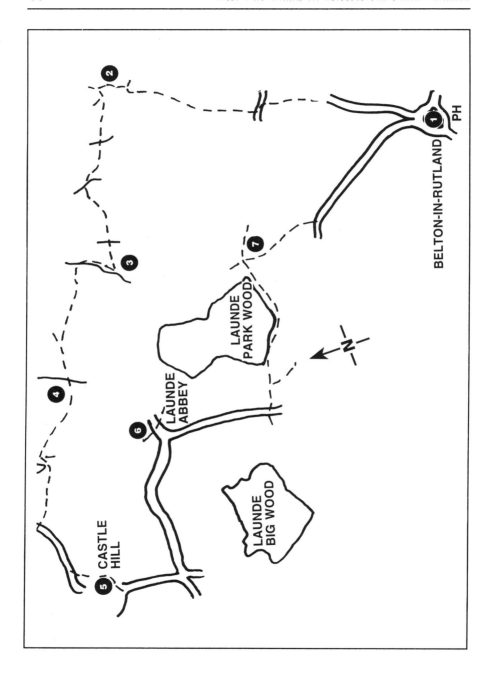

the route. For the full 10 miles turn right in the direction signposted to Braunston, which goes along the edge of the field with the stream to your left. 150 metres later three stone horse troughs lie abandoned under the trees, then a crossing farm track is met at the field edge.

Go down the hill with the hedge to your left, pass to the right of the rusted barn and through the gate. Head straight across, picking up the farm road by carefully unhooking the coiled-spring electric fence wire from its hook and then replacing it. The spring is quite strong, so be careful. Proceed along the road to Cottage Farm, cross the road, and take the bridlepath to Withcote past Avenue Farm.

4. The reason for the farm's name becomes apparent as you turn right through the gate and along a tree-lined track. At the end of the avenue the barn stands amidst a mass of slurry, which requires delicate negotiation. At the lake turn left and follow the muddy track around its perimeter until a double gate is met. Pass through the gate and continue up the tractor made road, probably amidst horses.

To your right Withcote Hall and its chapel lie in a picturesque setting. The Hall was built in 1723, but there were earlier dwellings on the site. The 15th century chapel was the private chapel of the Smith family, the owners of the land until it was confiscated at the restoration of Charles II because Henry Smith had been one of the Parliamentarians who had signed Charles I's death warrant.

Continue through two gates, pass Sauvey Castle Farm and go on to the main road. Turn left and go up the hill, being watchful for speeding cars, and noticing the pill-box to the right. Go down the hill, and as the road bends to the right, go left by the bridlepath sign and through the gate. Head right to the top of the field, ignore all the gates and turn left through the gap whose gate has disappeared. Keep the hedge to your right, parallel to the hedged stream some 30 metres to the left. Go past a horse-jump and trough, through a gate and then over the muddy bridge.

5. To your left lies Castle Hill, home of Sauvey Castle, the finest motte-and-bailey castle in the county to the tutored eye. It was built by King John in 1211 as a hunting lodge, abandoned in 1373, and now appears as a flat hill with a gash in it.

Turn right alongside the hedge to a gate, then head slightly left to another gate onto the main road. Go left, turning round for frequent glimpses of the castle as its shape becomes more apparent. At the crossroads go left to Launde, and at the brow of the hill pause and look back for the westward view. To the left is the flat-topped exquisitely-named Robin-a-Tiptoe Hill, whilst on the right Whatborough Hill catches the eye with its distinctive round-domed building. Continue past Abbey Farm and a motorcross course to Launde Abbey, where you rejoin the shortcut.

6. Launde Abbey is now a Retreat House and Conference Centre. The present building dates from the 17th century but was much altered in the 18th, the original Abbey having being founded for Augustinian canons in 1119. Little remains of the old abbey, which is private property anyway, but the chapel, dated c. 1125, is open on Bank Holidays from Easter onwards, Mondays throughout June, July and August, and Saturdays in August. The name Launde means a green level space between two woods, and that is a perfect description of this beautiful and tranquil spot.

   Turn right at the crossroads and go for over a kilometre towards Loddington, turning left by the bridlepath sign along the drive to Copt Hill Farm. When the farm road turns right, head straight along the dirt road towards Park Wood Farm, At a gate marked Private leave the road and continue through the black gate in front of you. Follow the hoofprints by the left-hand hedge to another gate, pass the farm and go through a further gate. Here the path is diverted along the side of the field and it can be slippery and chewed up by horses. Continue around the field, turning right at the end to a gate. To your right is a trig point, whilst to your left is a fine view of the early part of the walk.

7. Go through the gate and back into Rutland, then turn quickly right at the bridlepath sign and through a Leicestershire Round marked gate. Take the path downhill, which then heads left across the field. Ahead lies Belton, with Eyebrook Reservoir in the distance. Go through the gate, and then straight on, turning right with the edge of the field to a gate onto the road. A left turn takes you past the new cemetery on the 1.5 kilometre journey back to Belton, going straight on at the signposted crossroads to the war memorial. Turn right past St Peter's and into the Sun Inn to reflect on the glory of this outstanding walk.

11. PRESTON

Route: Preston – Martinsthorpe – Leigh Lodge – Ridlington – Preston

Distance: 8.8 miles, 14 kilometres or 6.2 miles, 10 kilometres. Quiet roads, good tracks with one indistinct section.

Map: O.S. Landranger 141 (Kettering and Corby)

Start: The bus stop by the Kingfisher pub, Preston on the A6003. Grid reference SK 872023

Access: Preston is 4 miles south of Oakham on the A6003. The Barton 2 and Fairtax Rutland Flyer give infrequent access from Oakham or Uppingham. Parking is possible in the village.

Fox and Hounds, Preston (0572 85492)

This attractive 16th century ironstone building has always been a pub. The smart lounge is abutted by a dining room, both low-ceilinged and oak-beamed, with a large fireplace in the eating area. A compact but well-designed public bar has a darts area, and the range of beers – Boddington, Pedigree, and a monthly guest beer – are all well-kept and offer a good variety of strengths and tastes. A wide range of meals at reasonable prices may be enjoyed.

Like many pubs of its age it is supposed to be haunted, in this case by a woman murdered in the 17th century. There is a garden, occasionally visited by a fox, and seats to the rear.

Open: Monday – Saturday, 11.30 – 2.30, 6.30 – 11; Sunday, 12 – 3, 7 – 10.30

Food: 12 – 2, 7 – 9.30

The Harrington Memorial, Preston

Preston

The golden stonework offset by neat verges are two of the reasons why Preston has won the tidy village contest several times. It looks and feels like an advertising person's dream, and repays close examination. The buildings to the north end are particularly attractive, but a walk down any side street is delightful.

The church of St Peter and St Paul is mainly 14th and 15th century, with Norman traces inside including a tympanum over the vestry door and massive pillars and arches around the nave.

The Walk

1. Turn right from the bus stop by the pub, taking the first right and then following the road as it bends right through the lovely village. Note the Fox and Hounds for future reference or even present delight, and continue onwards, eventually to the main road. Turn left down the verge, and as the road bends right look for a footpath sign on your left in the middle of a patch of nettles and brambles. If it is possible locate it and follow its direction over a fence into the field. If you don't fancy trying, walk down the road until you meet the farm track and use that for access.

Head down the hill, aiming for a gate in the end hedge to the right of the barns. This is not quite the right of way, which is not maintained or waymarked, but is the least damaging to the crops. Negotiate the gate, turning left along the field edge and then right at the corner. After 100 metres you meet an open gateway on your left which you go through, aiming towards a metal gate across the field, slightly to the right by a medium sized tree. Cross the bridge over the infant River Chater, from where you head up the hill with the hedge and fence to your right. This alleged bridleway is very indistinct, although the odd hoofprint will be met. Pass by Fox Covert with its old wall and continue to the top of the ridge, where climbing the wall on your right and jumping off seems the best way to negotiate the electric fence. I expect that the horses do the same.

2. Turn left to Martinsthorpe, the cemented up building being the former stable of the demolished Hall. Below it can be made out the earthworks of the deserted medieval village, whilst around it are a herd of frisky bullocks who are most curious about passers-by. Go round the far side of the stables to meet up with a stone farm track that soon becomes two cemented strips. The views on either side of this ridge are spectacular, Rutland Water to the rear contrasting with the empty space of the Chater Valley to the left.

    Cross the cattle grid, leaving your bovine companions behind, and stride out for about a mile as the track eventually becomes a metaled road.

3   When a crossing road is met, a left turn will lead to the shortened walk. If taken follow it to Ridlington, taking a stroll around the village to join the main route.

    Otherwise continue over, passing Hibbits Lodge as the road turns right. A left turn signposted Leigh Lodge is taken, passing some cottages on the way down to the lodge which is currently being renovated. Cross the bridge over the Chater, at which point my intention was to follow the footpath on your left which crosses a plank bridge, opposite to the signpost hidden in a tree on your right.

    I have travelled that path, which seems not to be walked nowadays, and in a couple of parts it requires a chainsaw, climbing skills and armour plating to get through. Hopefully it will be restored soon, but the alternative is far easier and to some extent better with its views to the south. Brave walkers may find it more interesting to see if they can find the original footpath.

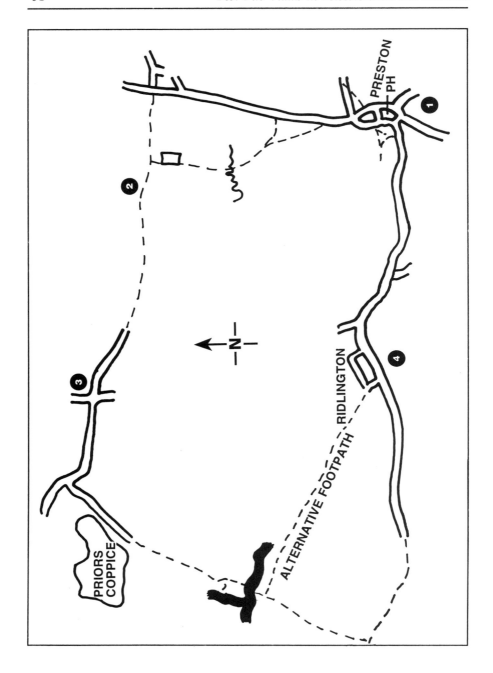

So continue along the track heading up the hill to the barn on the next ridge, where you turn left along the top to Wills Farm. There you join Holygate Road, presumably a reference to Launde Abbey at the western end, and follow it to Ridlington. A peek left through the gate opposite to Old Mill House at the start of the village reveals the top of the prehistoric earthworks.

4   Go left down West Lane, then right along Main Street. The village is publess since the 1950s, but contains many attractive houses. The old Post Office is a picture postcard building, whilst the church of St Mary and St Andrew has a lovingly maintained yard. Inside a Norman tympanum can be seen, and more unusually a case of musical instruments from the 18th and 19th centuries used in the church services. On the north wall of the chancel is a monument to the Harrington family, including James who was reputedly the organiser of the gunpowder and get-away horses for the Gunpowder Plotters.

Keep going down Main Street, passing an old pump and the neat village hall, before going right up East Lane. Turn left at the main road, forking right at the Give Way sign and following the lane to Preston.

On the outskirts of the village, 60 metres after the 30 mph signs, turn left up an unmarked path to the right of a green gate. This leads to the churchyard, and after a visit leave by the path through the wooden gates. Continue to the road, where you turn left to the Fox and Hounds. From there a right turn leads to the A6003 and the return bus or the Kingfisher.

12. NORTH LUFFENHAM

Route: North Luffenham – South Luffenham – Pilton – Wing – Lyndon – North Luffenham

Distance: 8.5 miles, 13 kilometres. (Quiet roads and footpaths)

Map: O.S. Landranger 141 (Kettering and Corby)

Start: Bus stop by St John's Church, Church Street, North Luffenham. Grid reference SK 935034.

Access: Luffenham is 2 miles south of Rutland Water and 5 miles west of Stamford, off the A6121. Several infrequent buses, of which the United Counties 12 from Uppingham – Stamford gives access on Monday – Saturday. Car parking is possible in the village.

Horse and Panniers, North Luffenham
(0780 720091)

The Nag and Bag, as it is known, is a grade II listed building, dating back to 1640. It was originally a bakehouse, but now the food is more varied and undoubtedly as tasty. The beers sold include an excellent pint of Everards Tiger, a testimony to the accuracy of the judges who awarded the pub a Best-Kept Cellar prize, and a guest beer. Bed and Breakfast is available, and the juke-box and other mechanical-noisemakers-free lounge adds to the pleasant atmosphere .

Open: Monday – Thursday, 12 – 2.30, 6.30 – 11; Friday – Saturday, 12 – 3, 6.30 – 11; Sunday, 12 – 3, 7 – 10.30

Food: Every day except Thurs, 12 – 2 and 7 – 9

North Luffenham

This mellow ironstone village has a long history, with excavations in 1863 uncovering a Saxon cemetery. Together with most of West Rutland it was part of the dowry of Queen Edith, wife of Edward the Confessor, which gives us the name of the nearby village of Edith Weston. Luffenham then passed through the Cecil family of Burghley fame into the Digby family, one of whom, Everard, was hung, drawn and quartered for his part in the Gunpowder Plot. According to local legend the plot was hatched in Luffenham Hall itself.

The latter is 16th century, and situated to the east of the delightful parish church of St John the Baptist. The church lies in a glorious setting; to the south lies the Chater Valley, to the west an old wall hides a playing field with an apparent dry moat or ha-ha at the end, whilst all around are magnificent walnut and yew trees. Inside is a memorial to Robert Johnson, founder of Uppingham and Oakham Schools, and quality mugs may be purchased for the church funds. In the rear graveyard are several stones of aircraft personnel from the nearby RAF camp, which is a major factor in the local economy.

Another famous inhabitant was Vincent Wing, who amongst other things was the author of an astrological almanac which was the best seller of its day, with over 50,000 copies sold in the 17th century.

The Walk

1. From the church bus stop turn right to the Horse and Panniers, then right again down Chapel Lane, left up Digby Drive and right at the junction to South Luffenham. To the left are many Christmas trees, and a disused windmill is perched on the hillside.

   Go under the Leicester-Peterborough railway, left at the junction and enter the village. Go first left down Gatehouse Lane, pass the Post Office and then right along The Street to the Boot and Shoe Inn.

2. Parts of this pub date back to the 15th century, and it has been a butcher's, a baker's, and a cobbler's. Perhaps the candlestick maker was too late to buy it. It is worth a look, and whilst you are there try the John Smith's.

   The most notorious resident here was a pupil at the Rectory School at the beginning of the century – Herman Goering. Rumour has it that the locality

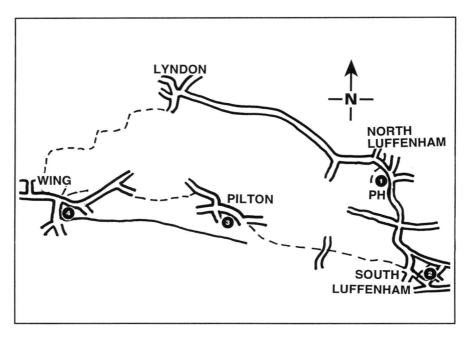

was spared bombing during the Second World War because Goering wanted to live in Burghley House.

Continue past the locked church of St Mary, whose neat spire abounds with crockets – the curly bits. Pass the phone box and turn right by the footpath sign along the narrow Church Lane. At The Square aim slightly left up Frisby Lane, then at the main road go right.

Pass West Farm, and when the road bends to the right continue straight on up a muddy unmarked bridlepath by the telegraph pole. Ignore the left turn, to Morcott, and follow the sign to Pilton.

To the right, North Luffenham is a picture, and to the left can be seen a windmill with full sails on the ridge.

Continue between the two fields, cross over an old telegraph pole, then turn right by an old tree stump through an iron gate, and then immediately left along the wide grassy path between hedgerows. Cross the road, noting the old earthwork to the right and carry on past Wymark Spinney. Two stiles are negotiated by horsejumps, as you proceed roughly in a straight line through a gate to the road. Go up the road, turning right at the crossroads to Pilton, and then left by the church.

3. The small church of St Nicholas has a simple 13th century doorway and a restful dignity. To the left a farm stable boasts over 250 horseshoes hanging on the nails outside, and as you proceed down the road have a look at The Cottage. 150 metres later as the road bends to the right, follow the footpath sign to Wing.

Go left for 30 metres, then right along the field edge. Pass through a crossing hedge by an oak tree, and head straight across to a path through some sunflowers. Continue on to the next hedge where the right of way is altered by an impenetrable rape field. Turn right along the hedge, then left with it to emerge onto a road. Turn left along the lane, right at the main road towards Wing and then take the first left signposted to the maze.

4. 40 feet in diameter, the turf maze is of unknown age and purpose. The design is exactly the same as that of the mazes laid out on the floors of Chartres and Poitiers Cathedrals, and several others exist in England. The most likely explanation is that it was used by penitents, who would progress around it on their knees, saying prayers at the junctions.

Return to the main road, where you go left. Pass the church and the Cuckoo before turning right down Middle Street, situated just before the Kings Arms. Go right at the bottom, then left by the footpath sign. Head downhill to a gate near the bottom of the right-hand hedge, cross the footbridge and go left then right along the railway edge. After 100 metres you cross the railway line by climbing the two gates next to signs telling you to be careful. Don't ignore them.

At the other side turn right along the field edge until the gravel path of a crossing bridleway is met. Turn left up the tractor path over the nascent River Chater, where you turn right through an old gateway into the woodland. Follow the path that goes to the left-hand fringe of the wood, where you turn right along the edge of the wood and then the hedge. Go left with the hedge, then right by a yellow waymarker. A further left and right leads to a small ditch and a gate, where you follow the path uphill. Turn left at the marker and then right along the field edge. This is followed for 600 metres in front of Lyndon Hall and then several elegant houses. The 17th century Hall has some 19th century additions and a handsome block of 17th century stables. At the road turn left to a signpost.

The rest of the village is very pretty, and a gentle stroll reveals much of interest. Alas there is no pub.

At the signpost turn right to Luffenham, carrying straight on along an open road at the top of the ridge. Excellent views over to Pilton may be had, but watch out for any overzealous pheasant shooters by the roadside. Proceed down the hill as the trees return to line the road, turning right at the junction along Church Street to the bus or pub.

The Horse and Panniers, North Luffenham

13. HUNGARTON

Route: Hungarton – Quenby – Cold Newton – Lowesby – Baggrave – Hungarton

Distance: 6 miles, 9.5 kilometres. Quiet lanes, good paths.

Map: O.S. Landranger 141 (Kettering and Corby)

Start: The Black Boy, Hungarton. Grid reference SK 690076

Access: Hungarton is 6 miles east of Leicester, 2 miles north of the A47. Very infrequent buses. Car parking is possible in the village or you might ask for permission to use the pub car park.

The Black Boy, Hungarton (053 750601)

Although the name is rumoured to have derived from an escaped slave who sought lodging here, it is most likely to have derived from the crest of the Burnaby family of Baggrave Hall. A further possibility is that it is named after a prince who was the "black sheep" of the family, and it is this image that adorns the inn sign leading to the apparent incongruity of the white face. The quality of the beer, Brew XI, Bass, Stones and Highgate Mild, has earned the pub several entries in the Good Beer Guide, and you will not be disappointed.

The well-appointed lounge and more functional Hungarton Bar give it the feel of a local rather than a passing-trade establishment, and you will receive a friendly and convivial welcome. Outside are two separate garden areas, with a range of playground equipment and picnic tables, and the food from the barbecue or in the bars is most tempting.

Open: Monday – Saturday, 12 – 3, 6.30 – 11; Sunday, 12 – 2.30, 7 – 10.30

Food: Monday – Saturday, 12 – 2.30, 7 – 9; Sunday, 12 – 2, 7 – 9

Hungarton

This attractive conservation village lies at the heart of the Quorn Hunt territory, which often meets at the Black Boy or one of the country houses which we pass on our walk. One famous active member is Prince Charles.

Much of the village was rebuilt between 1766 and 1775 by Shukbrugh Ashby, whose monument in St John the Baptist's Church gives testimony to the fact. The Ashby family owned nearby Quenby Hall, and there was an Ashby Arms inn in the village from the 18th century to the 1930s. The runners amongst you may care to note that the village hosts a 7 mile road race in July.

Quenby Hall

The Walk

1. Head downhill into the village along Main Street, turning left up Church Lane by the war memorial. The church is mainly 14th century and well situated with good views to the south, but may well be locked. Ignore the bridlepath sign to the left and continue downhill to a footpath sign pointing the way ahead between shrubs to the right of Brook Cottage. A stile and footbridge are passed, then you head off right across the side of the hill on a faint path that leads to the next footbridge. Cross it and turn left along a mown strip, turning right with it at the hedge and following it to the lodge on the hill.

Go through the gates of the driveway to Quenby Hall, the originals of which are in Leicester Museum, and proceed up the road. A pump is passed on the left, and the site of the medieval village of Quenby can be seen on the right with its bumps and hollows. As the road bends, the magnificent frontage of Quenby Hall opens up in front of you.

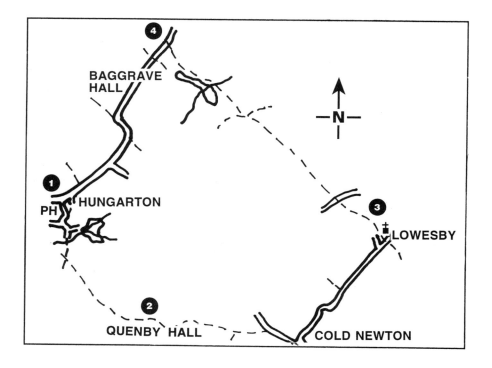

2. Quenby is, according to Pevsner, "the most important early 17th century house in the county". Built for George Ashby between 1620 and 1631 it had major alterations in 1767, but the Jacobean interior was reinstated in 1905. Here it is thought that Stilton was first made, by a housekeeper of Lady Beaumont.

    To the right of the house will be found a small gate, and you go through this and keep with the wall until arriving on the rear drive, a Land-rover track. This is followed for about half a mile to the road, with the densely wooded hill of Billesdon Coplow prominent on your right.

    At the road go right, and then first left into Cold Newton. The village green was donated by Squire De Lisle, the owner of Quenby, to commemorate Queen Elizabeth II's Silver Jubilee in 1977. Take the right fork and cross a cattle grid, noting the moated site to the right and continue with the undulations of the medieval village of Cold Newton all around you. This area cannot be ploughed, only grazed, and is unusual in that the grazing animals are pigs.

    Continue down the road through a couple of bends towards Lowesby, whose hall is apparent in front of you. Turn left just before the church into the graveyard by a footpath sign, going past the church and leaving by the far top corner of the churchyard. Cross over the drive of the hall, following signs and notices directing you left behind the far side of the fence. This leads around the edge of the grounds until eventually the front of Lowesby Hall comes into view.

3. The Georgian hall stands on the site of an earlier manor house, one of whose owners was Colonel Hutchinson, the Parliamentary Governor of Nottingham Castle during the Civil War. Many of the fine trees were planted by him. To the right is the site of the medieval village of Lowesby, which was re-located after the plague in the 14th century.

    Skirt the edge of the cricket field and then aim across the side of the hill parallel to the woodland below. As you come to the road a gate with the top bar painted white is obvious, and you go through it by a footpath marker. Head down the tractor road to the next gate, then leave it as it peters out near an old quarry and continue near the bottom of the field through two more gates. Pass above a yellow post, keeping parallel to the fence and then climbing slightly to round Carr Bridge Spinney. Drop down to the left to a gate and a crossroads signpost.

This is the sort of sign commonly found at road junctions, but this is at a crossroads of bridlepaths with not a scrap of tarmac in sight. Follow the signpost to Baggrave, climbing the stile to the left of the horsejump. Aim diagonally uphill, picking up a second stile by another jump. Go to the left of the large ash tree in front of you, passing through a small gate at the end of the field.

Pass over the gravel track from Bell Dip Farm above you, dropping down to the edge of the woodland by a newly fenced area. Continue to a stile in front of you, heading across the field to the next and then slightly uphill to the final stile that leads onto the road, where you turn left.

4. Baggrave Hall lies to the left of you, a 16th century building largely rebuilt in the 1750s. It is set amongst some impressive parkland, which contains perhaps the finest of the lost medieval villages that we have seen today. A recent owner of the hall was Asil Nadir, much in the news in 1993 for his donations to the Conservative Party, who could be found in the Black Boy on occasions.

The road bends left and right into an avenue of horse chestnuts, which leads to South Lodge. The view of Charnwood Forest to the right is worth a long look. Carry on down the road to the Black Boy and a welcome drink.

14. SWITHLAND AND BRADGATE PARK

Route: Swithland – Bradgate Park – Swithland Wood – Swithland

Distance: 6.3 miles, 10 kilometres. Good paths and open parkland.

Map: O.S. Landranger 129 (Nottingham and Loughborough)

Start: Bus stop by T-junction in Swithland. Grid reference SK 549132

Access: Swithland is 4 miles south of Loughborough. Frequent buses from Loughborough, Leicester and Derby on the joint Midland Fox – Bartons – Loughborough services 121 – 124. Car parking is difficult on the road, but possible near to the pub. Alternatively use the Bradgate Park car park at SK 542114 and start the walk from there.

The Griffin Inn, Swithland (0509 890535)

The pub derives its name from the crest of the Earls of Lanesborough, owners of the nearby hall. There are several rooms catering for different tastes, all of which will be stimulated by the range of beers on offer. Everards Beacon, Tiger and Old Original are complemented by Adnams, Old Speckled Hen, Bishops Finger and a guest beer.

The inn has been the hub of the village for three centuries. It has been used as a court and once as a mortuary following a disaster at the slate quarries – ghosts from which are said to appear from time to time. To the rear is about four acres of land with a trout stream and pool, with plenty of grass and picnic tables in this sunny south-facing area. Children, dogs and horses are welcome.

The Griffin also has facilities for traditional Leicestershire Long Alley skittles, which may be hired for the evening with or without a range of suppers. There is also Morris dancing on Boxing Day and the Quorn hounds meet here each year around about March. A wide range of meals

is available from their newly refurbished kitchens.

Open: Monday – Saturday, 11 – 3, 6 – 11; Sunday, 12 – 3, 7 – 10.30

Food: 12 – 2, 6.30 – 9 or 7 – 9 Sunday.

Swithland

The name is synonymous with slate, and the products of the quarries to the west of the village can be seen on many rooftops and in most cemeteries throughout the North Midlands. The Romans quarried here for use in Leicester, but the lighter Welsh slate began to dominate the market in Victorian times and the last quarry closed in 1887.

St Leonard's Church is usually locked, but the graveyard contains an interesting oddity. In the wall is the large tomb of Sir Joseph Danvers, partly inside the consecrated ground and partly in the gardens of the hall. The reason for this is that he lies buried in the hallowed ground, whilst his dog, which could not be buried there, can share his tomb by being buried alongside him but not in the churchyard. The carvings on the tomb are well worth examining.

His son John was an interesting eccentric, ordering all the doors, shutters and gateposts in Swithland and Mountsorrel to be painted red. He also took a fancy to the old cross at Mountsorrel and ordered its relocation at its present site in the hall grounds, replacing it in Mountsorrel by the rotunda that is so prominent today.

The village has a fair and fete at the beginning of September each year.

The Walk

1. From the junction, take the road east towards Rothley, passing the estate cottages to the Griffin Inn. Continue past it, noting the old school with its griffin crest opposite and the odd Tower House. Have a look around the churchyard, and then return towards the pub. On the bend before it there is a bridlepath sign to your left, which you should follow through the gate, where it turns to the right. It is well used by horses and obvious underfoot,

as we go along it for 500 metres to the road. Turn right, then immediately left up the tree-lined avenue to Cropston Leys.

Pass the house, and about 150 metres after the track becomes a narrow path, turn left along the path between the fields. As you enter the wood keep with the main right-hand path, go through a gate and down the grassy lane ahead. 200 metres later a signpost indicates the path to Bradgate Park. Go right over the fence and stile, aim slightly right to a second stile and then go diagonally across the field to a stile onto the road.

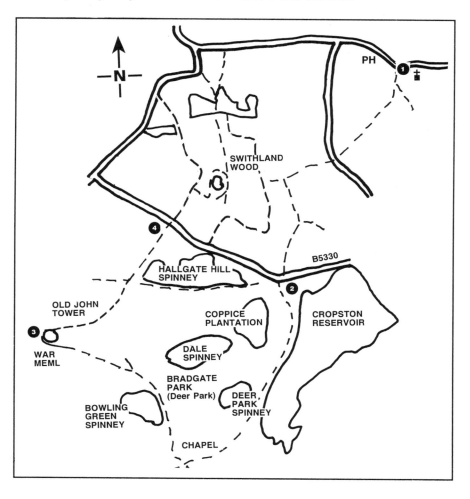

2. Cross over into Bradgate car park, and then into the Park itself. This can be busy and crowded, particularly on a summer Sunday, but there is plenty of space in which to wander and it is very attractive. The route now described takes in some of the highlights, but please feel free to make your own way depending on circumstances.

Bradgate has never been landscaped and retains the flavour of a hunting park. The rugged bracken and rock strewn hills are characteristic of the area, resembling a mini Lake District. One visit was on a bitterly cold and foggy December day, but the tops of the hills were above the fog layer and bathed in sunshine. With few people around it was idyllic.

Go along the tarmac road which runs parallel to the wall overlooking Cropston Reservoir, the wall having viewing slits for children and birdwatchers. To your right plaques denote firstly an oak planted for the 50th anniversary of the park, given by Charles Bennion to Leicester City Council in 1928, and secondly trees planted in 1946 to commemorate the Red Cross Agricultural Fund.

To your left both red and fallow Deer can be seen, as the road swings right towards the Chapel and ruins of Bradgate House, open to the public occasionally in the summer.

Completed in 1501, it was the home of the Grey family, the most famous of whom was Lady Jane Gray. She was manipulated by her father into a marriage, proclaimed Queen of England for 9 days on the death of her cousin Edward VI, and then deposed and executed at the age of 17. A sad end for an intelligent young lady who spoke six languages and was surprisingly well educated for a woman of her time. The house was abandoned in 1719 and has decayed to the impressive ruins that stand today.

Follow the house walls around and head up the hill, go through a gap in the wall and then pass by the wood to your left. As the path curves round you will see the War Memorial and Old John Tower on the hills above. Make your way up by any of the paths available.

3. The memorial is for the Leicester Yeomanry Regiment, and comAands a fine view to Charnwood. Go through the small walled wood and up to Old John, built from the remains of a windmill. This folly commemorates a servant who

Bradgate Park, war memorial

was killed when a pole from a celebratory bonfire toppled over on top of him in 1780. There is also a toposcope, pointing out the view, and a plaque to Charles Bennion.

With your back to the tower and looking at the viewfinder, go right down-hill and take a path left to a small pond. Continue on to skirt the wood in front of you by the Land Rover track below its left-hand side. At a small clump of trees turn left to a gate in the wall below, crossing over the lane and climbing the stile opposite. Go down this tree-flanked path to the road.

4. Cross the road and go through a gap in the wall opposite into Swithland Wood. Again you may wander freely or take the suggested route through the wood.

After 20 metres take the left-hand fork, following the path near to the wall as it climbs the hill. When a path emerges from the left through a gap in the wall, turn right along it, then left after about 100 metres up an old track. When you reach the top of the hill turn right to the strong fence surrounding the deep lake.

This is a flooded slate quarry, with an inscription just above the water indicating that the Leicestershire Rotary Club "secured the wood for a National Heritage" in 1931.

Continue with the fence to your right, turning right with it at the end of the quarry. When the fence again bends right, go down to a barrier across a path. The notice states that the bridlepath is closed to preserve the ground, but it may have since reopened to horses. Go along the bridlepath, downhill and away from the quarry. Follow it and its yellow markers, at rider height on the poles, ignoring any side paths.

A small clearing with a litter bin is reached, and as the path heads slightly uphill and left to a marker by a gate, we leave it by continuing down to a stile. This leads us on to a path between two fields, and we tread its delightful tree-lined way to the road. There a right turn leads to some bus stops nearby, or you may wish to continue up the road for about a kilometre to the Griffin Inn.

15. BURROUGH HILL

Route: Somerby – Burrough On The Hill – Burrough Hill – Somerby

Distance: 5 miles, 8 kilometres or 6 miles with diversion. Good paths, small amount of road.

Map: O.S. Landranger 129 (Nottingham and Loughborough).

Start: Bus stop by the Stilton Cheese Inn, Somerby. Grid reference SK 777106.

Access: Somerby is between Melton and Oakham, 4 miles west of the A606. Blands buses number 13, infrequent Melton – Somerby – Oakham. Car parking is limited but available on the High Street.

Stilton Cheese Inn, Somerby (0664 77394)

An attractive old building, built in 1665, serving Marston's Pedigree, Bass, Ansells and Tetley bitters by handpump. The lounge has a collection of stuffed animals and a welcoming fireplace. Seats are available outside.

Open: Monday – Friday, 12 – 3, 7 – 11; Saturday, 11.30 – 3, 7 – 11; Sunday, 12 – 3, 7 – 10.30

Food: At all times except Monday evening.

The Parish Brewery Inn, Somerby (0664 77866)

One of the few homebrew pubs in Leicestershire, recently moved for expansion from the Stag and Hounds in Burrough. The 16th century building incorporates a smart bar and a well maintained lounge, creating a pleasant atmosphere in which to sample the range of beers, our favourite being the Somerby Premium bitter which would grace any beer festival. Baz's Bonce Blower (O.G.1108) is the strongest ale on handpump in England, the Poachers Ale a dark 5.5% A.B.V. stomach-liner and the

Parish Special a lighter session beer. You may purchase all the beers in various sizes of carryouts up to 36 gallons, at a very reasonable price.

Brewery visits with buffet and beer included can be arranged at a modest fee, and there is also a garden, playground and outside seats.

Open: Monday – Saturday, 11.30 – 2.30, 6 – 11; Sunday, 12 – 3, 7 – 10.30

Food: 12 – 2, 6.45 – 9.45 except Sunday when 12 – 2, 7 – 9.30

Burrough Hill

The seven hundred feet high hill is crowned with an impressive Iron Age fort, giving an excellent view from the explanatory toposcope. The fort dates back to about 200 BC, with occupation likely to have been for 600 years, judging by the coins and pottery found. It probably had a timber palisade fence with strong gates, and was used as a place of refuge for the inhabitants of the surrounding countryside. Although the ditch has been partially filled, and the ramparts depleted for roadstone, it is nevertheless easy to appreciate how impressive a construction it must have been.

The Grand National was held here in 1873, although exactly where is not certain. Many will remember a more recent connection with the race in Burrough Hill Lad, the local horse who won the Cheltenham Gold Cup as well as being placed in the National.

An explanatory leaflet may be bought at Tourist Information Offices, and the notice board by the entrance is helpful. There is a car park at SK 767115.

The Walk

Note: If the Dalby Hills path is closed, the diversion adds about 1 mile to the walk.

1. From the bus stop go past the Stilton Cheese on the road towards Burrough Hill, along West End. By the bend turn left down the tree-lined road signposted Somerby Riding School, passing the stables, and after 100

metres, as the road turns left, go right through the gate to the right of the wooden electricity pole. Keep to the left of the field by the newly laid hedge, the path being clear and well-frequented by horses. Go through another gate and keep to the top of the hill, turning a little to the left.

When you encounter a line of gorse bushes, turn right downhill, then left at the bottom along the hedgerow. To your right is a small stream, and where another runs into this by the end of a single strand of barbed wire, a small plank footbridge is crossed.

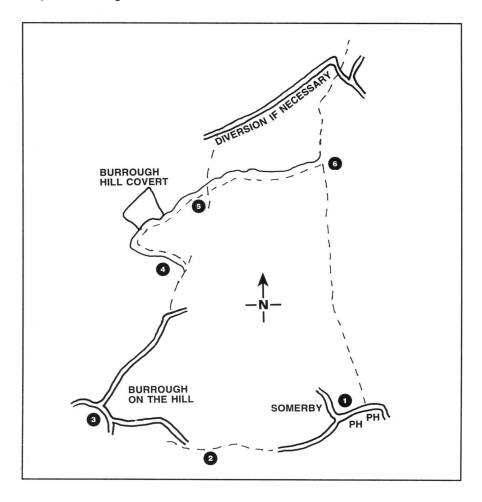

2. Turn left across the second stream, and go through the gate. Follow the path up the small climb, then turn right along the field edge. This is a diversion from the marked right of way, which goes to the post in the middle of the field, but it is the accepted local diversion. As you meet a cross hedge, either follow it left to the gap and then double back, or make the somewhat precarious crossing of the ditch by following the path down to an old wooden fence post used as a footbridge, and scrambling up the other side.

Continue around the side of the field by the right-hand hedge, which becomes a chainlink fence around the sewage works. Go up the concrete road to the tarmac, turning right past Burrough House into Burrough On The Hill.

3. At the green a short walk takes you to the Stag and Hounds, well worth a visit for the Lloyds Stag bitter, exclusive to the pub, and the range of guest beers which are often from small breweries. A few hundred metres further on past the pub is Burrough Court, where the Duke of Windsor first met Mrs Simpson. Unfortunately the house burnt down in the war when it was requisitioned for troops.

Our route lies to the right, along the road to Somerby. On the way we pass the church of St Mary, its picturesque tower and clock featuring as the Parish Brewery symbol, where there is a memorial to Sir Raymond Greene. He was a distinguished officer, politician and keen huntsman, who resided at Burrough House. When he died his ashes were spread on the rockery by his butler using a silver spoon. He was related to the novelist Graham Greene, and grandson of the founder of Greene King Brewery.

Continue along the road out of the village with a good view to the left of the toposcope on Burrough Hill. After 800 metres turn left over a fence by a footpath sign, just past the roadsign for the car park. Follow the concrete tractor path past the Severn-Trent building, climb the fence at the end of the hedge and take the path across the next field to the modern gate or the old concrete v-stile, emerging onto the sandy road. Turn left to the information notices and the hill fort.

4. Go up the path to the earthworks, turning left along the top to the toposcope. On a clear day Lincoln Cathedral can be seen 43 miles away, but in all weathers the viewpoint is dramatic. Continue with the clockwise

circuit around the surprisingly large top, with Burrough Hill Covert to your left. This woodland forms the boundary between the Cottesmore and Quorn Hunts, and the upper parts are open to the public.

At the end of the wood, as the earthworks turn right, go down the hill with the woodland fence on your left. Climb the hill opposite until a double gate is met, with yellow markers indicating the Dalby Hills path. Go through the gates and follow the excellent path until a large sign indicates the private section of the path.

5. This is usually open, at the discretion of the Ernest Cook Trust who own the land, but it will be occasionally closed, as it was on our visit on December 31. Please respect their right to close it, and if necessary take the alternative route which is no less interesting.

Should the path be open, then simply follow the markers until at the end of a small woodland, (6) on the map, a sharp right-hand turn through a gate is indicated.

The diversion involves dropping down the hill by the fence in front of the wood for 50 metres to a small gate. Go through the gate and follow the bridlepath across the field to the road near Home Farm. Turn right along the road, passing Hall Farm after 1 kilometre. To the left Little Dalby Hall and church can be glimpsed through the trees, and are worth a quick visit up the signed path. The road bends sharply to the right, and we quickly turn right by a signpost to Somerby.

Head diagonally across the field, aiming towards the left of the copse next to the wooden buildings, crossing the stile by the yellow marker. Follow the path to the next stile, and head up the tractor track in front of you to a further stile into a muddy field. Stick by the left-hand fence until reaching the woodland, then aim slightly right to the stile and gate where we rejoin the Dalby Hills path.

6. Cross the stile and go up the lane, noting the cross-country course to the left. Climb the next stile and head straight up the hill past the yellow post to the stile on the skyline. Follow the Leicestershire Round sign, the walk from Burrough Hill to Somerby being part of the Long Distance Footpath, and head across the field on the well trodden path. Somerby church tower is conspicuous in front of you, as you cross the next footbridge and attendant

stile, following the path over the next field to the stile. The path now goes by a hedge, then heads across to a further stile, where you may see some excellent examples of scarecrows on the horizon.

Cross the small field, rounding the top of a stream to a waymarked stile in the wooded area. Continue with the hedge on your left to the top of the field, turning right for 20 metres to yet another stile. Climb over this one and go between the trees to a stile, from where you head downhill, slightly to the left of the prominent weather vane on the primary school.

A further four stiles are crossed, roughly in a straight line, before coming out into an alleyway which leads to Somerby.

The village has an interesting church, unusually with a central tower, and was the birthplace of William Cheselden. He was one of the fathers of English surgery, and attended Sir Isaac Newton on his deathbed.

To your left is the Parish Brewery, and to the right the Stilton Cheese. Don't waste time dithering, try them both. Heads you go left, tails you go right.

16. EXTON

Route: Exton and its park.

Distance: 4 miles, 6.5 kilometres. Private roads and good paths.

Map: O.S. Landranger 130. (Grantham).

Start: Fox and Hounds, Exton. Grid Reference SK 925112.

Access: Exton is a mile north of Rutland Water, off the A606 Oakham to Stamford road. Access by infrequent Cottesmore bus services from Melton, Oakham and Stamford. Limited parking available near the pub.

Fox and Hounds (0572 812403)

This imposing, creeper-clad building was a 17th century coaching inn. The high-ceilinged interior brings to mind a hotel rather than a local, yet the atmosphere manages to incorporate the finest elements of both. A wide variety of meals may be had in the bar or restaurant, whilst outside the tables in the well-maintained garden overlook the attractive countryside, with good views to the south. There are few better places to sit with a pint of Samuel Smith's or Pedigree on a sunny day, and we would recommend that you visit after the walk or else you may not quite summon up the energy to leave.

Open: Monday – Saturday, 11 – 2.30, 6.30 – 11;
           Sunday, 12 – 2.30, 7 – 10.30

Food: 12 – 2, 6.30 – 9.00

Exton

A beautifully-maintained Rutland village, thatched stone houses nestling around the sycamore-shaded green. A gentle stroll reveals all sorts of nooks and crannies, but perhaps the most interesting area is that around the Old Hall and the church of St Peter and St Paul. A leaflet in the church gives details of the impressive monuments to the Noels and Harringtons, and the mighty marble sculpture of Viscount Campden by Grinling Gibbons. These are amongst the most important 16th to 18th century church carvings in England, a marvel of detail. Outside, the ruins of the hall, burnt in 1810, lend a romantic air. Please note that the grounds are private, with access to the church only by the narrow road.

Exton holds a locally famous street market on the last Monday in May.

The Fox and Hounds, Exton

The Walk

1. From the pub turn left and then left again down Barnsdale Avenue towards the main road. After 150 metres a private driveway on the right gives access to the church of St Paul and St Peter, (2); after visiting it return to the pub.

   Head to the right of the green up Stamford Road, and at the right-hand Give Way sign go straight across to the cul-de-sac Field Road. Pass some new

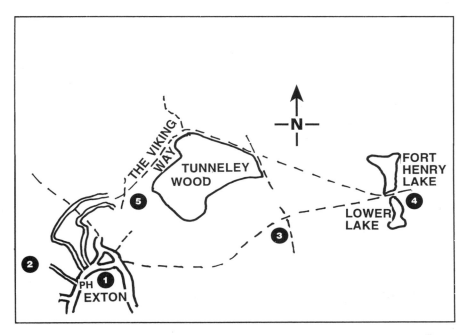

houses and go through the gate by the side of the cattle grid into Exton Park. Follow the tarmac road, cross a cattle grid and enjoy the extensive views towards Stamford. At the fork in the road, go straight across up a wide green bridlepath, (3), which is not signposted. Continue on to the road down to the lake, where fishermen and wildfowl mingle in serenity.

4. To the left can be seen Fort Henry, a Gothic summerhouse from the early 19th century, finely landscaped to the left-hand side of the lake. A pair of binoculars will enable you to enjoy its pinnacles and terrace, as well as the variety of waterbirds. Return up the road, ignoring our earlier path and a right-hand side road. Pass a barn and a left-hand road to pass to the right of Tunneley Wood.

At the wood's end turn left onto part of the Viking Way, then take the right-hand fork. At the next junction turn right for a hundred metres or so for a good view into the new hall and its cedars. Return, and carry straight ahead crossing a further cattle grid. At the next grid go right by a Viking Way sign and along a road by some thatched cottages. Turn left and then right by the old butter cross, looking like a medieval bus shelter, on to the High Street and down to the Fox and Hounds.

17. WHISSENDINE

Route: Whissendine – Ashwell – Teigh – Whissendine

Distance: 8 miles, 13 kilometres.

Map: O.S. Landranger 130 (Grantham)

Start: The White Lion, Whissendine. Grid reference SK 830142

Access: Whissendine is 4 miles north of Oakham. The infrequent Barton 2 Nottingham to Oakham and Blands 304 Melton to Stamford give sufficient time to do the walk, but only just enough for a quick pint. Car parking is possible in all villages.

The White Lion, Whissendine (0664 79233)

This old inn is now knocked into one room, but it nevertheless retains separate and distinctive areas. The restaurant has a good selection of meals, the lounge is comfortable and relaxing, and the public offers devil amongst the tailors, bar skittles and pool. The range of beers available include Everard's Tiger, Beacon and Old Original, Ridley's IPA and Wadworth's Farmers' Glory. Early in July is feast week.

The highlight, certainly in summer, is the beautiful garden by the river. It contains picnic tables by the willows, and has a collection of ornamental birds and rabbits including a white peacock. With a small children's playground it is very suitable for families.

Open: Monday – Saturday, 12 – 3, 6 – 11; Sunday, 12 – 3, 7 – 11

Food: 12 – 2, 7 – 9.30 or 10 on Friday and Saturday

Whissendine

This long village is built around the main road, and until 1867 belonged to the Sherrards of Stapleford Hall. To the west is a seven-storey high mill, the second tallest in the country, which was built from the walls of Stapleford Park when they were demolished because they were "keeping the fox's in". At the opposite end of the village lies the old Manor House, surrounded by somewhat mutilated earthworks and hidden in the trees.

Nearby the church of St Michael and All Angels, a monstrous "village cathedral" built by Joan, Princess of Wales, in memory of her husband the Black Prince. The 14th century tower is highly regarded, and the screen in the southern aisle originally adorned St John's College, Cambridge who received it as a gift from Margaret, wife of Henry Tudor.

One parish custom still held today is that of "Letting the Banks", an area of land. Each March a candle is lit, a pin placed in it, and the last person to bid before the pin drops is allowed to graze sheep and horses on the Banks for a year.

The White Lion, Whissendine

The Walk

1. From the White Lion turn left towards the church, passing the Three Horseshoes, now owned by Belhaven, on the way. Ignore the left turn to Stapleford, and continue around the right-hand bend on the road to Ashwell. Pass Samafika House, and as the road goes left continue straight on through an iron gate up the bridleway to Langham and Burley. Surprisingly extensive views can be had as you walk for about half a mile in a fairly straight line. When the hedge to your right finishes, at the end of the corn field, turn left with a crossing hedge to your right. It is easy to miss this turn as the bridleway continues slightly right as well, but look out for a low Winged Fellowship marker which, although not pointing in our direction, is a useful guide.

   The path can be muddy and slippery as it narrows between old hedgerows, due in part to motorcycles, but it is passable with care. At the road turn left, continuing over the railway to the main road. Turn right here, then left down Brookdene by the Village Hall. At the end turn left, and then left again at the main road to the church of St Mary.

2. The church may well be locked, but it is worth going into the churchyard to see the tall cross to the south west of it. Although the inscription has faded, it marks the grave of the Reverend James Adams, the first clergyman to win the Victoria Cross. This was for saving the lives of men in the Afghan Wars in 1879, after which he became an honorary chaplain to the Queen before moving to Ashwell.

   The village no longer has a pub, so press on, leaving the churchyard by the overgrown steps to the north. Turn left, then right at the crossroads along Teigh Road. This can be busy but it has wide verges containing a good variety of flowers including some unusual poppies. As you come into Teigh note the bridleway on your left, to which you will probably return after visiting the church. Continue, going left with the road before taking the first left-hand turn, just before the green, to the church of Holy Trinity.

3. If the church is locked, a key can be obtained near by, and it is highly recommended that you do so. Inside is a unique "Strawberry Hill Gothic" pulpit from which the parson preaches some 13 feet above ground level. Since this is at the west end of the church, the pews are arranged facing

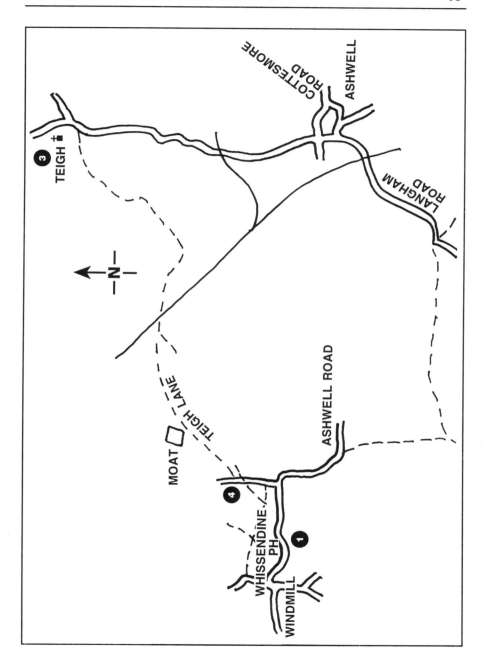

inwards so that the congregation can see both ends with ease. It feels like being in Parliament.

A splendid guide-leaflet gives more details, including some of the people connected with the church such as Anthony Jenkinson who was the first Englishman to penetrate Central Asia. There is also a brass inscription set up as thanksgiving for the return of all 13 of the villagers who served in the Great War. There are only 31 such villages in England, and Ashwell is the only one in Leicestershire.

There are two possible routes from here. Either leave the churchyard by the north side, going past a topiary animal of dubious parentage, and then taking the first road left to the green and then left to the bridleway, or leave by the gate from which you entered and turning right to the footpath sign. I have not walked this footpath, but it is shown on the maps and certainly at the far end is well marked as it crosses a field. It should be straightforward, but if not please contact the county council and not the publisher.

For those now back at the bridlepath, go right down it, passing the Caravan Club site, and continue for a mile as it changes from a bare earth road to an overgrown grassy path. It is good underfoot and not difficult to walk. Just before you come to the railway crossing the footpath joins from the left. Cross the line to Teigh Gate House, with its attractive gardens and noisy menagerie. Watch out for the geese if they have young, but don't be worried by the Alsatian who is allegedly a big softy.

Continue down the lane, passing a brick pillbox which looks reassuringly incongruous today. Just after a look through the hedge to the right will reveal the old moated manor site, with the earthworks plainly visible and still containing water in parts.

4. At the main road turn left, pausing for the view over the village to the mill, and then take the second footpath on the right by the sign opposite to the hidden Manor House. This leads into a field containing Highland Cattle, but they are very docile and will watch your passing impassively. Keep by the left-hand hedge to the stile, from where you aim to the right of the house in front where a metal gate is found. Head down to a footbridge in front of you, then up to the right of the wind pump where you climb the fence by the corner. From there go to the stile opposite, pass through a pleasant garden and up the drive to the road. Turn left, passing a cattery, and then left again at the main road to the White Lion.

18. COPT OAK

Route: Copt Oak – Oaks in Charnwood – Bardon Hill – Copt Oak

Distance: 7 miles, 11 kilometres. Good paths, some roads.

Map: O.S. Landranger 129 (Nottingham and Loughborough)

Start: The Copt Oak pub. Grid reference SK 483129

Access: Copt Oak lies 4 miles east of Coalville, near the M1. By bus, the Midland Fox 121 Leicester – Loughborough gives you about 4 hours to complete the walk with its twice-daily service, Monday to Saturday. Local Coalville buses give access to the Greenhill Estate, point (5) on our map at SK 458143. Car parking is limited in Copt Oak.

The Bull's Head, near Coalville (0530 810511)

The notice outside tells you that at 787 feet this is the highest pub in Leicestershire. The low-ceilinged oak-beamed L-shaped bar serves Tetley's, Ansell's, Burton and Marston's bitters in a relaxed and convivial atmosphere. Outside the road entrance is an old petrol pump, whilst around the back are picnic tables and a children's playground overlooking the open countryside. The lunchtime food is good value, and popular with local workers and travellers. Children are only catered for outside in the evenings and at Sunday lunchtime.

Open: Monday – Saturday, 11 – 2.30, 6.30 – 11 (summer) or 7 – 11 (winter); Sunday, 12 – 3, 7 – 11

Food: Lunchtimes except Sun, filled rolls otherwise.

Copt Oak

A small cluster of houses by the M1 is not the greatest advert for this excellent walk, whose strength lies in the variety and quality of scenery. Nevertheless, Copt Oak has a nice name, meaning "enclosed oak", and surprising interest.

The Bull's Head, Copt Oak

The church was one of three built in the early 19th century, when the Enclosure Act accelerated the transformation of the Charnwood area from the hunting preserve of the lords of Groby, Whitwick and Shepshed. The architect, William Railton, was also responsible for Trafalgar Square. There is a popular pub, dispensing Marston's Ales, and the old school of 1839 is now a Youth Hostel.

An old pump has been renovated, a plaque by it stating that in times of drought a designated keeper stopped people using it outside of specified times by his blowing of a whistle.

The Walk

Warning: Bardon Hill Quarry may close the road to the top during blasting, Monday – Friday, 12.15 to 1.00, and Saturday, 11.45 to 12.30.

Please bear this in mind and alter the direction of your walk if necessary.

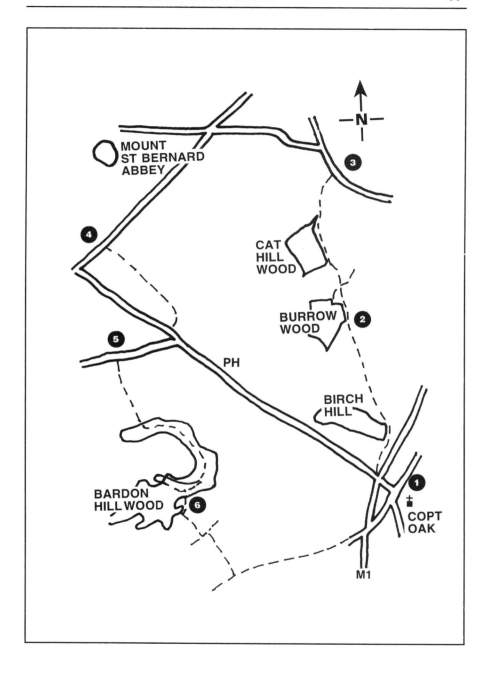

1. From the pub turn right past the Hostel, then right again past the pump. Go left over the M1 and at the end of the bridge turn right down the bank and over a signposted stile.

   Follow the right-hand fence over two more stiles, then head slightly to the left around the walled wood. A cow track heads down diagonally across the field to a stile by the corner gate; cross over the lane and enter the field by scrambling over the dilapidated gate, now probably collapsed, or wall. Head left to a gap in the hedge, walking in a direction just to the right of the pylon in front of you. Climb a stile and maintain your direction along a path to a gate.

   To your left the moorland of Timberwood Hill is most striking, whilst the noise of the M1 is greatly diminished by the hill to the right. Go through the gate and aim slightly left to the stile opposite, then go downhill towards the far corner of the field diagonally and over the next stile into the edge of Burrow Wood.

2. Cross the stream and stile into a field whose undulations indicate the site of some old long-gone buildings, possibly the old convent at Charley. To the right Charley Hall peeks out through the trees, but we stay at the top of the field keeping the wood on the left for about 100 metres until turning left through a gate by a white painted path sign.

   Continue with the fence and stream to your right, and when it turns right, head off to the left of the solitary hawthorn tree. About 70 metres above the bottom gate of the wood in front of you is a path notice, rather faint besides the stone stile. Cross into the wood, follow the well-trodden path, exit through the gap in the wall opposite and follow the left-hand wall and signs through three fields.

   Go over the stile into the thin strip of Cat Hill Wood, following the yellow markers on the trees which lead you across it to a further stile. Head diagonally across the field, passing a green post and new stile the sometimes swampy Mires to a stile, and hence to the road.

3. Turn left and then first left to Oaks in Charnwood. The church of St James the Greater is well situated and lovingly maintained. Inside on the wall are six lances from the Battle of Waterloo which occurred on the same day, 18th June 1815, as the church was consecrated. Continue up the hill, Ives Head

and its trig point standing out well behind the church, whilst on the left an old horse-drawn caravan lies sadly neglected near a barn.

At the road junction go left, though if the Belfry Hotel has reopened then a pint can be had by going straight on for a couple of hundred metres. Be careful along this busy road which is rather narrow in places and without a footpath. The tower on the right belongs to Mount St Bernard's Abbey, founded in 1835 and still very much in use by the Cistercian Order. It was the first Monastery built in England since the time of the Reformation.

After 1 kilometre pass High Tor Farm, with some curious buildings to your right in the woods, and 200 metres later turn left over a stile into Warren Hills Nature reserve. The triangular marker with red inlay is the sign for the "Geological Walks in Charnwood Forest", an informative leaflet available at libraries and Tourist Information Offices.

4. Take the main path slightly left of the rocky tors in front, pass between two old gateposts and follow the wall or the skyline path straight on to a stile and then down to the road. Turn left and go past the road to Coalville to the Bull's Head.

Return to the junction and turn left down the hill towards Coalville. About 30 metres after passing Romans Crescent turn left by the footpath sign, (5), going between houses, up Vercar Close and then slightly left to a footpath and gate. The footpath around Bardon Hill has been rerouted. Purists who wish to follow the old route should note that the ability to hover 50 metres up in the air will be necessary for crossing the expanded quarry.

Go straight up the path to the woods, and turn left along the broad track. Follow this as it skirts around the bottom of the wood, going right with it past a cross-country course. After a kilometre a metaled road is met, where you turn right and climb to the top of Bardon Hill, at 912 feet the highest point in Leicestershire. Although rather cluttered by transmitters, there is a good view across the Midlands from the summit trig column.

Go back to the top of the road where a narrow footpath threads its way to your right and steeply downhill. Follow it until you emerge at a Geological walk sign by the old farm buildings.

6. Cross the stile and go right along the path to a private drive, crossing a further stile slightly to your right. Climb another stile, cross a precariously

bendy footbridge and accompanying stile. Go down by the ditch to a road, where you can go right should you wish to extend the walk and see the moated Old Hall Farm, but we go right then quickly left through a gate. Follow the arrows around the edge of the field, emerging through an old gateway by a house.

Turn left along what was the boundary of Bardon Deer Park and follow the path along the field edge. To your right Old Rise Rocks stand out, but we continue towards the transmitter by Copt Oak.

When you climb a stile into the road, go straight over the opposite stile and follow the fence. Cross a double stile and then follow the path, kindly restored by a considerate farmer who marks it with his tractor wheels after ploughing, and over another stile. Aim slightly right to a stile half-way along the fence, climb up the embankment to the road and turn left to Copt Oak.

Warren Hills

19. BEACON HILL AND WOODHOUSE EAVES

Route: Woodhouse Eaves – Broombriggs Farm – Beacon Hill – Buck Hill – Jubilee Woods – Outwoods – Woodhouse Eaves

Distance: 7 miles, 11 kilometres. Popular, well-marked paths.

Map: O.S. Landranger 129 Nottingham and Loughborough.

Start: The bus stop by the Pear Tree and Forest Rock pubs, Woodhouse Eaves. Grid reference SK 532142

Access: Woodhouse Eaves is 4 miles south of Loughborough. Hourly Midland Fox 121 – 124, Derby – Loughborough – Leicester, Monday to Saturday. Parking available in Woodhouse Eaves or in the various car parks met on the walk.

Curzon Arms, Woodhouse Eaves (0509 890377)

An attractive garden with plenty of tables serves as a pleasant frontage to this interesting pub. It has been a pub for over 200 years and was originally called The Anchor. Its name was then changed to the Beumanor Arms in 1947, but that only lasted for 2 weeks as they realised that there is no coat of arms for Beumanor in Leicestershire. The present title is taken from the Curzon-Herrick family who owned the land.

The tiled public bar is simply furnished, with a recessed darts area and welcoming fireplace, and perhaps better suited to walkers than the comfortably upholstered lounge. John Smith's Bitter and Courage Director's are available through handpumps, and a wide range of meals and bar snacks can be purchased, including a children's menu and pensioner portions. The pub also has a sandpit for the youngsters to bury you in.

Open: Monday – Saturday, 11 – 2.30, 6 – 11; Sunday, 12 – 2, 7 – 10.30

Food: 12 – 2, 7 – 9.30

Woodhouse Eaves

A picturesque village with many stone cottages roofed with the local Swithland slate. It has a collection of up-market restaurants and inns, attracting people from a wide area for the evening. The walk passes by several attractive gardens, but none more so than the rockery in front of the War Memorial, arguably the finest in the County.

The church of St Paul stands proudly on the rocky hill overlooking the village. It was designed in 1837 by Railton, who was also responsible for the Albert Memorial and the other two Charnwood churches, mentioned in the Copt Oak walk.

We also pass 1 Victoria Road, originally called Liberty Hall, built by Maurice Levy who used the balcony to address the villagers in his role as Liberal Agent at election time.

The Walk

1. From the bus stop go past the Forest Rock Inn and uphill, with the church high up to your right. Notice the unusually named Dun Caning across the road, presumably a retired schoolteacher's house, as you pass the war memorial and church entrance. Turn right by the bus stop after number 34, through two iron barriers onto a tarmac path. Continue to the top of this path, going right at the end down Victoria Road.

   The houses at the end are worth perusing before you turn left up the main road towards Maplewell. After about 250 metres a gate appears on the right, just after number 98, leading onto the Broombriggs Farm Trail.

2. This has been set up by the owners, Leicestershire County Council, with the aim of fostering a better understanding of the work and problems associated with farming. There is a series of information boards covering a wide range of topics, and we shall pass ones describing crop rotation, soil, the view, grasses, hay making and wall building.

   Go through the gate, and after 70 metres turn left over a footbridge. We now follow the yellow rectangular signs, turning left at the end of the field uphill by the side of the wall and woodland. Pass the first information board,

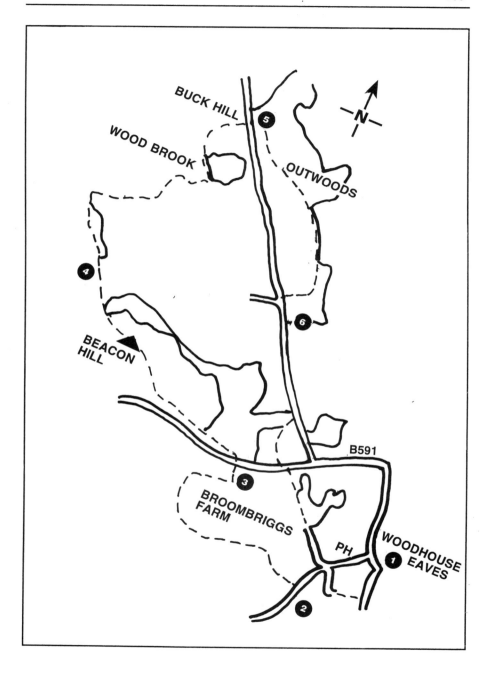

cross two stiles in quick succession and then a further stile. Here you go left around the edge of the field, through a gate and left again along the wall and fence. Pass through another gate, turning left onto the farm drive and from there to the main road.

3. Cross over the road and go through the gate into the Beacon Hill Park, taking the left-hand fork signposted Beacon Hill Upper Car Park. When the summit looms into view, slightly to your right, take any of the paths leading up to the top where the toposcope indicates the surrounding hills and sights, from High Cross in the south to Nottingham in the north east.

    The earthworks at the top are probably Bronze Age, certainly relics of that era have been found there, and it is a prime site for fossils. The rocks are 700 million years old, mainly composed of layers of volcanic ash deposited under water, tilted, and then compressed 600 million years ago to form the local slates. A leaflet is available giving more details from Tourist Information Offices.

    From the toposcope head to the Ordnance Survey Column and continue in the same direction to the cinder road. Cross it and go through the gap in the wall by the post, on the back of which can be seen the red and green triangular sign of the Geological Walks in Charnwood leaflet, (G.W.). Take the path to the outcrop, and go downhill to the left-hand edge of the evergreen wood in front of you. Follow the G.W. markers left and then right as the path skirts the conifers along an avenue of beech trees to a gate marked Jubilee Walk.

4. Take the permissive footpath opposite into the woods. The way ahead is obvious and well marked, turning right after the stream crossing and proceeding alongside Wood Brook. Go through two gates, then right over a footbridge. When you come to a junction with several paths, take the left-hand one alongside the wall which then turns sharply left. The path then climbs up the wooded Buck Hill, emerging into the open on top of the narrow ridge.

    In front of you Nanpantan Hall is well sited as you descend Leicestershire's equivalent of Striding Edge; well, maybe a small Cat Bells perhaps. Turn right at the bottom, go through a gate and then cross the stile into the wood. Go right alongside the wall and then go through two gates to the road.

5. Turn right and then after 20 metres go left through a gap in the fence into Jubilee Woods. There is a bewildering array of unmarked paths in here, but as long as you remain roughly parallel to the road you can choose your own way. The described route is one possibility amongst many.

Enter the wood, and after 20 metres turn right. Follow the path for 250 metres until a wire cross-fence is met. Go left along the wide path beyond it, until you meet a plaque embedded in a rock. This commemorates the opening of the plantation by Prince Charles in 1985, and also the memory of the founder of the Men of the Trees.

50 metres after the plaque turn right along the path next to the wire fence. Pass three benches close together and a wood store, continuing in the same basic direction. A curiously shaped and much abused beech tree is met, a small stream crossed and the Outwoods Nature Trail is joined by post 24 at the corner of a stone wall and open field. Keep going on with the wall on your left, with a view to Loughborough opening out.

When the wall turns left, go with it and then immediately right along the edge of a newly cleared area of woodland. Hopefully the path will have recovered from the logging machinery as you go past posts 16-13, turning right past 12 and 11 to the road.

6. Go left down the road towards Woodhouse Eaves, turning right after 1 kilometre into the Beacon Hill Lower Car Park. Cross the car park towards the notices and pay box, taking the large left-hand path with the yellow rectangular waymarkers. At the top of the rise you will find two picnic tables, where you leave the markers and aim slightly left downhill by the side of the stone wall.

At Beacon Road turn left, then cross over into the Broombriggs Farm Car Park, noticing the Leicestershire Round sign. Take the left-hand gate and go straight ahead with the fence to your right. Pass through another gate, aiming slightly uphill to a yellow marker, and pass through a gate into the right-hand fringe of Windmill Hill Wood.

You can climb the hill to see the base of the old windmill and for the view, otherwise continue along the bottom of the hill, eventually joining a tarmac lane to Maplewell Road. Turn left down the hill to the Curzon Arms, and afterwards continue to Main Street where you turn right to the start of the walk.

20. REARSBY

Route: Rearsby – Rotherby – Hoby – Rearsby

Distance: 5.6 miles, 9 kilometres. Good paths.

Map: O.S. Landranger 129 (Nottingham and Loughborough)

Start: Packhorse Bridge, Rearsby. Grid reference SK 652145

Access: Rearsby is 7 miles north east of Leicester on the A607 to Melton. The Fairtax X1 Leicester to Melton gives excellent access, and other buses are available. Parking is available in any of the villages.

Blue Bell, Hoby (0664 434247)

This 17th century thatch-roofed inn was originally three cottages, but now has two rooms: a neat, mainly dining area, and a more open lounge with photographs of guide dogs that the pub have sponsored, a collection of bank notes and numerous jugs and mugs. The meals available include a good selection of home-made food, whilst the beers cover the full range of Everard's output although only the Original appears to be cask.

Outside the pub the merit of the hanging baskets and floral displays has led to the pub being finalists in the brewery's garden competition, and there are picnic tables in the large grassy area with probably the best selection of children's playground equipment in the area. There is also a skittle alley for hire.

Open: Monday – Friday, 12 – 2.30, 7 – 11; Saturday, 11 – 3, 7 – 11; Sunday, 12 – 3, 7 – 10.30

Food: Wednesday – Thursday, 12 – 1.30, 7 – 9; Friday – Saturday, 12 – 1.30, 7 – 9.30

The Blue Bell, Hoby

Rearsby

Although it is now a quiet village, especially since the bypass has been finished, Rearsby used to have a substantial knitting industry with over 70 frames in operation in the 1830s. The focal point is the packhorse bridge, known as Seven Arch Bridge, which was constructed in 1714. Tradition has it that it was completed by six men in nine days, which is rather reminiscent of a maths problem; if it takes six men nine days to build seven arch bridge, how many men ...

The church of St Michael is of 13th century origins, but was reclad and restored in the 19th century. Amongst the slate gravestones is that of Cleare Sacheverell, who was evicted from the rectory in 1644 for his Royalist sympathies. His uncle Andrew was also buried here in 1658, but a century later his leaden coffin was dug up and sold for 28 shillings to buy the clerk a coat.

Although not met on the walk, it is worth seeking out Mill Road and looking at number 2, Rearsby Old Hall built in 1661, and number 8, the Old House from 1610. There are two pubs on the old A607 serving the village.

Seven-arch bridge, Rearsby

The Walk

1. Depending on the bus used, you may have to walk into the village to find the Seven Arch Bridge on Brookside. Cross the bridge towards the church, going from there along the path skirting the church wall to the right and then turning left. Go down Church Leys Avenue for 50 kilometres before turning left by a Leicestershire Round (L.R.) sign up a metaled path. This crosses a field, with a convent to the left, before meeting the road to Thrussington. Do not go up it, but cross over to Wreake Drive and after 80 metres go left by the L.R. signpost up the path to the stile. Aim diagonally right to a gate leading over the railway and into the field, where you turn right and follow

the embankment. Pass through a gate, then go left at the field end by a waymarker.

Go right by the sign at the riverbank, through a section of burdock and other tall plants, and then left across the bridge over the Wreake. Head along the embankment to a second bridge, after which you keep to the left-hand fence and pass the old mill. The path leads between two barn-like buildings onto the farm road. Follow this through two slight bends, then 50 metres after the "Private No Fishing" signs turn right before a hedge to a nearby pylon. There is a footpath sign in the hedge to the left of the road, but it is rather hidden in the overgrown hawthorn.

2. The path goes to the right of the pylon and a stile, then goes through fields of barley and corn before a hedge is met which accompanies us to our left. Cross a stile and keep by the hedge, passing an L.R. sign on the way to another stile. Aim for the yellow posts to the left of the brick house in front of you, then go around the house and along the drive to the road.

Climb the stile opposite, taking the path through the pea field to the double fence, turning left with the path to the stile. Continue to the ash tree in front of you then turn right along what remains of the avenue to cross a stream by a cartbridge. A stile lies to the left in the hedge which leads to a road, where you turn left to Hoby.

Just before the road junction Rooftree Cottage is met on the right, a cruck-framed cottage whose garden was open to the public on the day that we visited. Go right to the church of All Saints, noticing the truncated cross now bearing a sundial on the left of the path. The church is 13th and 14th century but usually locked, so continue through the churchyard and head up the road to the Blue Bell.

3. Return towards the church, soon taking the left-hand footpath by the L.R. sign to Frisby. The narrow path winds between some old cottages to a footbridge, from where you go diagonally left towards a yellow post. This leads on to two kissing gates either side of a bridge, from where you aim right to the bridge over the Wreake. This is on the site of the old mill, bits of which can be made out around the area.

Go through the hedge and straight across the railway. Follow the right-hand hedge to the next post where you leave the L.R. by turning right to the

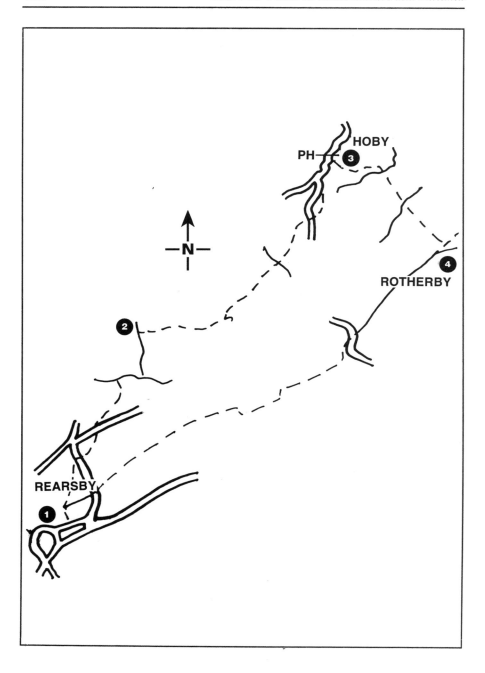

bullock pens. Either go through them, if they are unoccupied, or climb the fence to the road where you go right.

4. Rotherby contains some impressive houses but no pub. On your left the Rotherby Wildlife Garden has a picnic table from which you can observe the pond and its inhabitants. Pass through the village and over two cattlegrids to Brooksby, whose hall was once the seat of the Villiers family. Lord Cardigan, leader of the Charge of the Light Brigade at Balaclava, lived here after the Crimean War, but it is now the Leicestershire Agricultural College.

Turn right at the road then quickly left along the drive between two hostels for the college. Keep to the left of the church, which is worth a visit for the Villiers monuments, passing to the left of the 1992 dated herb garden. Go to the left of the cottage, where a yellow marker and stile can be found hidden under the trees. Keep to the right-hand fence and the faint path until the next marker comes into view in front of you.

Climb the stile and go on to the next one which includes a small gate at the top to make access easier for dogs. A farm track is picked up which leads to the farm, where you turn left and then right by the sign to Hive's Farm, with the piggery on your right.

Go down the stony track, going right and left with it. At a crossing lane continue over a stile, and when the left-hand hedge ends go through the gap and continue up the obvious path opposite. Pass through the kissing gate at the end, with the hedge on your left and then climb the stile by the fence to your right. Some impressive new houses and one genuine Georgian mansion are encountered as you make your way to the road, turning left and then right up Brookside to the packhorse bridge.

21. WALTON ON THE WOLDS

Route: Walton – Seagrave – Walton

Distance: 5.6 miles, 9 kilometres. Good paths, quiet lanes

Map: O.S. Landranger 129 (Nottingham and Loughborough)

Start: The Green, Walton on the Wolds. Grid reference SK 593198

Access: Walton is 4 miles East of Loughborough. The Midland Fox 138, Melton to Loughborough, passes through Walton, but times are largely unsuitable. The same bus has a better service to Burton on the Wolds, 1 mile north of Walton, or you can use the Barton 12, Nottingham to Leicester along the A46 to 1 mile south-east of Seagrave. Car parking is possible in the village.

The White Horse, Seagrave (0509 814715)

A quiet two-roomed local serving good beers in the Marston's Pedigree and ordinary bitters, together with Banks Mild. The lounge has a welcoming fire and a collection of Hunting photographs, and the larger public bar is equally attractive. Outside there are tables to the rear, where the barbecue is served, a garden where children are welcome and a petanque court. To the side of the car park is the old stable, now a listed building, which hosts the ghosts who reputedly play dominoes in the bar during the early hours of a quiet morning.

Open: Monday – Friday, 11 – 2.30, 6 – 11; Saturday and Bank Holidays 11 – 11; Sunday, 12 – 3, 7 – 10.30

Food: Light bar snacks at all times. Barbeque Easter – October. Saturday, 7 – 10.30, Sunday 12 – 2.30 and Bank Holiday Mondays 12 – 9 including Christmas

Walton on the Wolds

This small village has maintained its heart, the village green, and what new building there has been is largely harmonious and unobtrusive. One 600 year old house, Kingscote, was, according to local legend, the shelter of Richard III on the eve of the battle of Bosworth Field. He must have had several doubles, judging by the number of places he allegedly stayed, drank and ate that day.

One famous native of the village was Augustus Hobart-Hampden, better known as Hobart Pasha. Born in the rectory behind the church, he had a successful naval career before becoming a blockade runner for the South in the American Civil war. Pasha is a Turkish title, bestowed on him for his work as an Admiral in the Ottoman fleet and later as commander of their Black Sea navy in the Russo-Turkish war of 1878. The Anchor Inn takes its name from his exploits, and one of its bars is named Hobart's Cabin. There you may sample Burton and Tetley beers and traditional English home cooking.

The church of St Mary was built in 1739 on the site of the ruined St Bartholomew's. In the churchyard lie the base and steps of a cross of unknown age, whilst opposite the Manor has an enormous if sickly-looking cedar in its front garden.

The Walk

1. With your back to the Anchor, head uphill along the main road opposite, Black Lane, towards Seagrave. Take the second right along New Lane to the church. Continue along the lane, and as it turns right, go left through a gateway along the signposted bridlepath. When the lane opens out into a field, take the tractor path which heads slightly right before straightening up towards the opposite side of the field. There a gateway leads onto an old grassy lane, and when the next field arrives maintain the direction alongside the hedge.

   Cross the next field to a bridge over Fishpool Brook, ignoring the footpath to the right, and continue through the gate and along the obvious path. To the left an old house is starting to crumble, whilst to the west the views of Charnwood Forest and Beacon Hill in particular catch the eye. Continue through two more gates to the road.

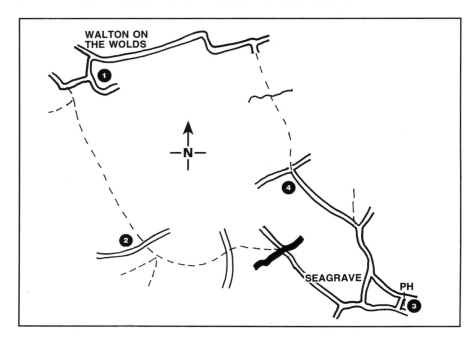

2. On your left are the Quorn Hunt kennels, built in 1905, solid brick buildings with a touch of the Victorian Gothic style. Cross the road and go up the bridlepath opposite. After 150 metres the bridleway turns right through a gate, but we turn left through a gap in the hedge and then right along the edge of the field. This is a diversion from the marked right of way, but seems locally accepted.

At the top of the field go through the gap in the hedge, then turn left alongside it. Continue until you meet a new stile leading onto the road to the gypsum works, not marked on the older maps and 1:50,000 series. Climb the stile opposite, where the arrow indicates the direction of the right of way. However most people go right along the fence, climbing it as it turns left and then going left yourself alongside the tree-fringed stream. In the far corner of the field a concrete bridge leads across a tributary and onto the road.

Turn right and walk the 1.6 kilometres into Seagrave, taking the left-hand fork and then the second left down Church Street to the White Horse.

3. After refreshment enter the churchyard of All Saints. If the church is locked,

peek through the window by the south porch for glimpses of the Norman font and the serpent. The latter is an early 19th century musical instrument, housed in a glass case above the north doorway and named for its shape. A previous Rector here was Robert Burton, author of the bestselling Anatomy of Melancholy.

The weather vane is in the shape of a fish, used during the plague years to indicate that a freshwater spring was here.

Seagrave reputedly derived its name from the burial place of King Seg, hence Seg's grave, whose estate included Seg's Hills now called Six Hills. The village gave its name to the Seagrave family who came to prominence in the 12th century when Stephen Seagrave, a monk, supported King John against the Magna Carta. He rose to become Chief Justiciar for Henry III, persuading the King to eliminate some of his loyal supporters, before Henry realised who his real enemy was and confiscated many of Seagrave's estates.

By contrast his grandson Nicholas Seagrave stood at the side of Simon de Montfort in battle, becoming a member of the first true parliament. He was later taken captive at Evesham, but eventually became reconciled with King Edward and accompanied him on the last Crusade.

Keep going to the end of Church Street, turning left at the end past the Post Office. At the road junction head right along Green Lane, and take the first left up a road unsuitable for vehicles. Pass Rose Farm and follow the right-hand fork, Muckle Gate Lane, until the main road is reached.

4. Go through the double gate slightly to the right of straight opposite, by a footpath sign. Again the right of way is diagonally right across the field, but when the crop is growing it seems considerate to use either the edge of the field or one of the tractor paths across it. At the far side, between the right-hand tree and the corner is a large gap in the hedge. Go through and head downhill by the left-hand hedge to the familiar concrete bridge over Fishpool Brook.

Turn left, then right along the hedgerow. Emerge through a gate onto the road, where you turn left and follow it to Walton. On the way you see some attractive houses and gardens, one of which contains the statue of a small gorilla.

22. HATHERN

Route: Hathern circular

Distance: 4 miles, 6.5 kilometres. Meadow land.

Map: O.S. Landranger 129 (Nottingham and Loughborough)

Start: Bus shelter on A6 at the north end of the village. Grid reference SK 499223.

Access: Frequent buses from Loughborough, Nottingham and Derby. Car parking is available in the village.

Three Crowns (0509 842233)

This quiet local has three separate drinking areas, and a well used long-alley skittle room to the rear. The back garden used to be an orchard, but now only one pear and one apple tree remain. The tiled public bar is lively and welcoming, with a collection of bottles adorning the walls. A selection of draught Bass beers is on sale, usually including two different milds, Bass and Worthington bitters. A barbeque is held on August Bank Holiday, but otherwise tasty rolls, and on Saturdays burgers, are the only food available. The co-licensee, Meg Gibson, is a U.S. citizen.

Open: Monday – Thursday, 12 – 2.30, 5.30 – 11; Friday, 12 – 3.30, 5.30 – 11; Saturday (Sept – May) and Bank Holidays 12 – 11 pm, else 12 – 3, 7 – 11; Sunday, 12 – 3, 7 – 10.30

Food: See above

Hathern

The old village still retains much of its charm, with the area around the church of St Peter containing much of interest. The ancient cross has its original steps and lower part of the shaft; the top broke off in a gale in

Normanton-on-Soar church

1916 and was repaired in 1920. A 16th century half-timbered house nestles on the edge of the churchyard, and the church itself, whilst much restored, has a Saxon font and some interesting characters associated with it. Rev. Andrew Glen was a noted 17th century botanist, and Rev. E Phillips was rector for 51 years. A leaflet is available in the church, as was home-made jam when we visited.

Hathern, its name deriving from haegthorn or hawthorn, was also the home of John Heathcoat who invented a brilliant lace-making machine. When he set up in nearby Loughborough his machines were destroyed by the Luddites, causing him to flee to Tiverton where he prospered.

The village takes great pride in its prize winning band, which has been going for well over 100 years.

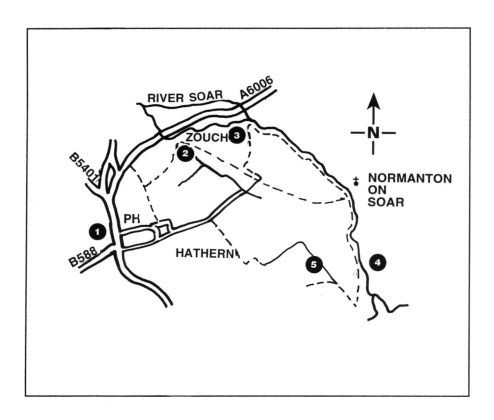

The Walk

1. From the bus stop on the village side of the A6, turn left and then left again down Narrow Lane. At the cross turn left into Church Street and carry on to the church. Go right down Green Hill, then left by the Catholic church into Green Hill Rise. Continue along the lane, with the cemetery on your left, and go right at the footpath sign and yellow waymarker. Pass a substation, and then head slightly left by a marker to an obvious new stile. Cross a field to the next stile, roughly in front of a white cabin. Go over the stile and right along the track to the River Soar.

2. 50 metres later, turn right to climb another stile, aiming for the stile opposite across the undulating field, an indication of the medieval strip farming methods that used to occur here. Go over the stile, keeping by the hedge to another stile, where a path joins from the right. Cross this stile and head on to the stile opposite, ignoring the local's short cut path to the left which is not a right of way. Climb the stile, trudge on by the hedge and over a final stile into a lane. Turn sharp left, returning in the direction from which we have just come. At the signpost turn right alongside the hedge, cross the bridge, and then follow the path left to a stile in front of a strange grey metallic structure. Traverse the stile to the river, where the structure is revealed as a new lock at the junction of the Soar and the Zouch Cut. It is possible to cross the weirs here for a pint in the Rose and Crown in the Notts part of Zouch.

3. We now follow the river upstream for about a mile, crossing several stiles, with the attractive houses and gardens of Normanton on Soar on the opposite bank. To the right markers indicate the fences on a cross-country or point-to-point course, and we will meet some of them at close quarters later. After the end of Normanton we go under some electricity cables, and then cross an old stone footbridge and stile.

4. Carry on for about 100 metres before turning right across the meadow along a tractor or Land-rover track to the corner of the field. Turn right just before a yellow post, and then right again alongside the ditch, effectively heading back parallel to the river. Cross a footbridge, (5), and aim slightly right of straight ahead towards two trees, the right-hand of which is covered by a mature ivy plant. A yellow post can be seen, to the right of fence 10, where we turn left and go straight across the field to two signposts. Turn right

along the hedge, cross the footbridge and stile to your left and keep by the field edge. After the next bridge turn right, and follow the obvious path past the football field and Band Headquarters to exit over a stile into a lane.

Turn left, then take the first right over the tarmac covered Green. Go left up Green Hill, noting on your left the old village pinfold or cattle pound, now built into a garden wall. Pass the church and go on to the Three Crowns with its distinctive sign. After a suitable break, continue up Wide Lane to the main road, turning left to the bus stops.

23. PRESTWOLD

Route: Cotes – Hoton – Burton on the Wolds – Prestwold – Cotes

Distance: 7.5 miles, 12 kilometres. Good paths, one section indistinct.

Map: O.S. Landranger 129 (Nottingham and Loughborough)

Start: Cotes Mill, Cotes. Grid reference SK 554206

Access: Cotes is 2 miles north-east of Loughborough on the A60. Frequent Midland Fox 99 buses, Loughborough to Nottingham go through Cotes and Hoton. Loughborough station is 1 mile away from Cotes. Car parking is limited at Cotes on the main road, but possible on the side roads.

Cotes Mill, Cotes (0509 231786)

This unusual pub was converted from the last working watermill in the county, used for grinding animal feed up until 1773 and then flour until 1950. In 1861 it was the scene of a fatal accident when Thomas Kettleband, an ancestor of Spike Milligan, caught his arm in one of the mill's wheels and subsequently died. Unusually, his ghost is not said to haunt the place.

The mill was converted into a pub in 1978, and now sells Everard's Tiger, Old Original and Mild alongside the Adnams Bitter. The inside rooms have a comfortable feel and good views over the countryside, whilst outside there are seats in the attractive garden.

Open: Monday – Friday, 11 – 3, 7 – 11; Saturday, 11 – 3, 6 – 11; Sunday, 12 – 3, 7 – 10.30

Food: Bar snacks at lunchtimes. Restaurant Friday and Saturday night, Sunday lunch.

Prestwold

During this walk we skirt the delightful grounds and obtain good views of Prestwold Hall, once the seat of the Packe family but now yet another conference centre. Sir Christopher Packe, Lord Mayor of London and a staunch Roundhead bought the estates from the newly impoverished Royalist Skipwith family, and his monument may be seen in the restored church. The house was largely rebuilt in 1760, with the exterior made fashionably Italianate in 1842 for C.W. Packe, whose initials may be found on the datestones of many of the estate buildings in Hoton.

Prestwold Hall

The Walk

1. From the Cotes Mill turn right and follow the A60 towards Cotes Village. After 150 metres the road bends sharply to the left, and 50 metres later as it bends to the right climb the left-hand fence by the remains of an iron gate. Go up to the raised area, and follow the edge of it to a stile.

   The path from here is indistinct and diverted by the central enclosed area. Essentially go straight across to the gap in the brick wall, and walk through the ruins until turning right down the track to a gate onto the road. The remains are of the Old Hall, built in 1580, but abandoned by the Packes in favour of Prestwold after a fire in the early 18th century.

   At the road turn left, and after 800 metres go right at the bridlepath sign, a slight reroute from the map.

2. Keep along the track below Moat Hill, then follow it uphill, as directed by the yellow waymarkers. Continue along the track, well-used by local riders, to a right turn by a hedge and then left at the next. Carry on for two kilometres, passing below Rigget's Spinney.

   To the left can be seen Stanford Hall, splendidly situated on the hill. The hall is now owned by the International Co-Operative College, and boasts an interesting theatre with an organ that rises from the ground, one of the few left in the country. It is worth a visit regardless of what play is on. Also to the left can be seen the white Rempstone Hall, situated like Stanford in Nottinghamshire.

   Ignore a farm track to the right, following the yellow post to the next marker where we turn right along an old muddy lane towards the now disused Hoton Church.

3. At the A60 go right to the Packe Arms, and from there continue to the bend where you carefully cross over towards the estate cottages dated 1853. Look back towards the church, a curious hybrid of styles and repairs.

   An interesting diversion is to walk for 100 metres down Wymeswold Road, where some old cruck-framed cottages can be seen alongside a restored barn that gained a Charnwood District award for conservation in 1989. Return to the church and go down Vinetree Terrace on your left, turning

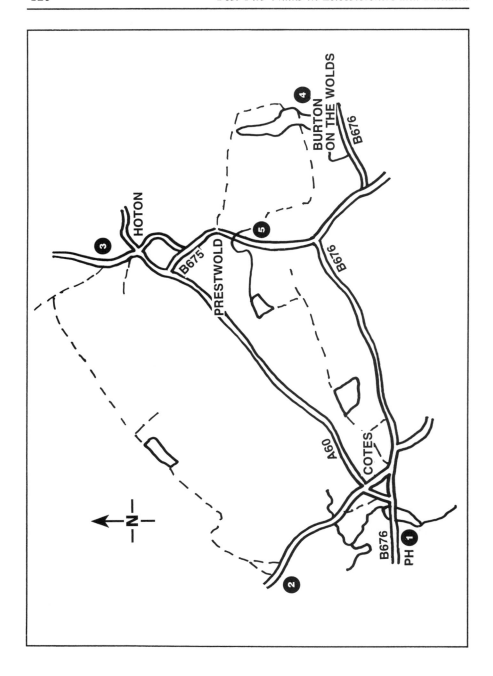

right along Old Parsonage Lane. Pass a kennels with colourful wall decorations, and go left along the road towards Prestwold.

To the left lies the abandoned Wymeswold Airfield, now apparently used for go-kart and similar racing, judging by the tyre walls.

At the bend go left as directed by the footpath sign, cross a stile by the cattlegrid and follow the left-hand hedge. Eventually you pick up some yellow markers which direct you through a gate and between two rows of concrete posts. Continue past the old hangar, cross a footbridge and soon head up a bank.

Turn right along the path at the top as it winds through the brambles, past a post and into a narrow lane between hedges.

Cross a stile, and proceed along the path straight across the field.

At the end you have to negotiate a steep-banked ditch, which can be slippery. Alternatively a bridge can be found 200 metres to the left. Go right, then left at the field edge by Old Wood, a diversion from the map. Proceed through two gates across the old green road from Prestwold Hall to Seymour House.

4. Here you may turn left if you wish to Burton on the Wolds and the Greyhound Inn, a five minute walk. If so, return to this spot.

   Turn right to a yellow waymarker, following the path through Old Wood as it emerges along a stream. The views of Prestwold Hall across the fields are particularly good when the afternoon sun picks out the colour of the southern aspect, and the box and yew trees surrounding the church make it most photogenic.

   Cross the stone bridge as directed, then go left before coming back sharply to the right along the footpath to the churchyard. Exit by the opposite gate, and follow the signs through the woods, listening for green woodpeckers amongst many other bird species, and going through three gates to the main road.

5. Turn left by the old Sunday School, and go right by the footpath sign, again a rerouting from the map. After 60 metres turn left along the hedgerow by a small stream, then after 100 metres go right along an old metal fence in front of some newly planted trees.

At the end of Big Spinney turn left along the tractor path, going right at the next hedge along a well signposted path. This goes on for 1.5 kilometres past Mere Hill Spinney, down to a yellow post where you turn left to the main road. At the road turn right and continue to Cotes Mill, or turn right down Back Lane to the crossroads at Cotes.

Cotes Mill

24. BUCKMINSTER

Route: Buckminster – Coston – Sproxton – Buckminster

Distance: 8 miles, 13 kilometres. Old roads, fieldside paths.

Map: O.S. Landranger 130. (Grantham).

Start: Bus shelter at Buckminster. (Grid reference SK 878228).

Access: Buckminster is 8 miles east of Melton Mowbray on the B676. The infrequent Barton bus number 10, Oakham or Melton to Grantham and the Saturdays only Skinner bus 141 from Saltby to Leicester both visit the village. Car parking is possible off the main road.

Crown Inn, Sproxton (0476 860035)

This late-19th century stone building masks older roots, incorporating 16th century stables at the rear which have been used as a mashroom and a slaughterhouse at various times. A warm welcome from Rosie Pearce and Graham Atkins, two of the youngest hosts in the country, is guaranteed in the snug bar with its old church pews, sewing machine tables and valuable high backed pew. The latter is very much a fixture of the place because, since the alterations were done, it will not be possible to take it out. A good selection of food is available, either in the bar or the restaurant where booking is advisable. The beers on sale are Marston's Pedigree, and Everard's Beacon bitter and mild. Outside can be seen the old fire insurance plaque high above the doorway, whilst at the back is a boules court, barbeque area, seats and a playground. A large aviary is an unusual feature of interest to bird lovers.

Open: Monday – Friday, 12 – 2.30, 7 – 11; Saturday, 12 – 3.30, 7 – 11
Sunday, 12 – 3, 7 – 10.30. Occasionally open all day on Saturdays.

Food: 12 – 2, 7 – 10.30

Buckminster

An attractive village, the green between the church and the former stables of the Georgian hall being a particularly pleasant spot. The church of St. John the Baptist is interesting without being spectacular. Its first rector was Baldric in 1222, and it soon passed under the patronage of the Knights Hospitaller of St. John who were based at Winkhill in Notts. The 15th century font is nicely carved, a sundial outside has the words "such is life" intriguingly written above it, and there is the large Mausoleum of the Earls of Dysart close by. They are the Tollemache family, the local landowners, whose name is taken by the large village pub.

The Tollemache Arms is very much the hub of the village, the lounge with its hunting prints complementing the cosy bar with its signed photographs of Frank Bruno and Gary Lineker. At the time of our visit it sold Boddington and Featherstone beers from handpump, the latter at a very cheap price. A variety of meals are available. At the west end of the village is a variety of presumably estate housing, including a terrace of sixteen cottages from about 1850.

The Walk

1. Take the Sproxton road from the west end of the village, and after 300 metres, as the road bends to the right, turn left through a blue double gate, (2), on to a track. Follow this track with the hedge to your left, and when the track disappears keep going in a straight line until a yellow waymarker is met 800 metres later.

   Follow the direction of the arrow straight across a large field, exiting by a small footbridge onto the B676. Turn right, and when the road soon turns left, continue along the minor road in front of you. After 100 metres this road turns right, but you go up the farm track of King Street lane in front of you. Proceed for a kilometre to the bottom of the valley, turning left on the minor road towards Coston. Avoid the ford by the bridge to the left, or have a paddle if you feel like it, and turn right at the main road to Coston church.

3. The church of St Andrew sadly shows signs of neglect and was locked at the time of our visit. This was a pity because inside there is an unusual

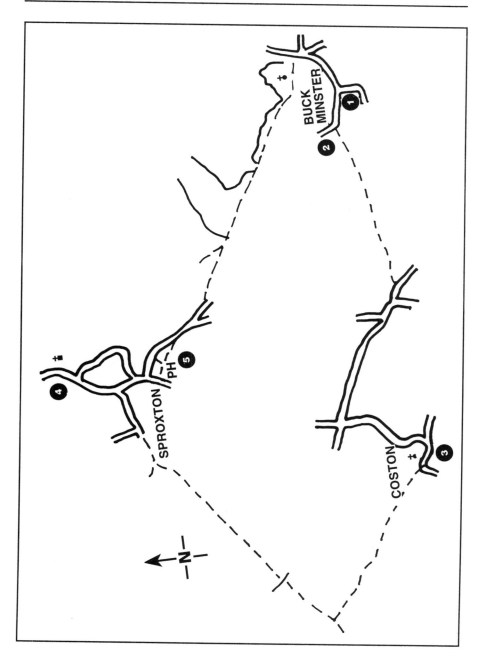

plaque to Temple Crozier, the actor son of the rector, who was accidentally stabbed to death during a play called "Sins of the Night" in 1896 in London. As his death coincided with the final curtain, the audience left unaware of the tragedy that they had witnessed.

From the church continue along the road, and as it turns left keep straight along the narrow lane by the modern Manor Farmhouse. Keep straight on for 800 kilometres, and as the tractor path starts to bear right, go past a blue gate and turn left along the bridlepath next to the hedge. This comes to a T-junction with a second bridlepath by some newly planted oak trees, and there you turn right.

When you come to King Street lane again turn right and immediately left – effectively straight on. To your right the covert of Sproxton Thorn, locally known as The Thorns, shelters pheasant and fox, whilst overhead you may well observe gliders and the towing plane from the nearby airfield. The path continues in a straight line towards Sproxton church, visible on the skyline, passing over a stream in a delightful valley before joining a minor road. Continue up the road to Sproxton, turning left at the T-junction and up the hill to the church.

4. St Bartholomew's is magnificently situated, with extensive views to the west. Its main treasure is a Saxon Cross, rescued from its former role as a footbridge, outside the south porch. Three sides are ornately carved, the fourth having been worn smooth by the passage of thousands of feet, and there is a creature called the Anglian Beast climbing up to the top.

    From the church start as if to return down the hill, but turn immediately left instead along Church Lane. Take the first turning right, and at the bottom of the hill turn left to the Crown Inn, located up the side street to the right.

5. On leaving the pub turn left, then left again between two old houses, numbers 2 and 3, and follow the yellow waymarker by a metal gate. Cross a stile and turn left to a gate by a water-trough. Go through the gate and aim diagonally right across the field, emerging at a stile and bridge over a ditch to the road.

    Turn right, take the left fork towards Buckminster, and after 100 metres a prominent yellow waymarker on the left indicates a footpath across a wheat field. This path had recently been ploughed and was consequently absent, but the farmer assured us that it exists and is obvious in summer. The path heads towards a second waymarker at the corner of the wood by the edge of Buckminster Park, and you then go right with the fence to your left. Continue along the wood edge, cross a stile followed by two others in quick succession. Good views into the park are to be had, and there are innumerable pheasants with partridge and the odd woodcock.

100 yards after the third stile aim slightly to the right across what is usually a sheep field to a waymarker next to a gate. Go through the gate and up the lane to emerge by the church. After a visit head up along the green to Haley House, where you turn right to the Tollemache Arms.

25. BREEDON ON THE HILL

Route: Breedon – Melbourne – Breedon

Distance: 3.9 miles, 6.3 kilometres. Good paths.

Map: O.S. Landranger 129 (Nottingham and Loughborough), and 128 (Derby)

Start: The bus stop by the Lime Kiln pub. Grid reference SK 407228

Access: Breedon lies on the A453 near Donnington Park and Airport. The infrequent Barton 3C Nottingham to Melbourne, Stevenson 176 Coalville to Loughborough and Paul James 100 Castle Donington to Ashby give a good service Monday to Saturday.

The Holly Bush Inn, Breedon (0332 862356)

The original low-ceilinged, oak-beamed bar of this 16th century inn exudes a cosy and warm atmosphere. It appears to have once been 3 cottages, now joined into a long and narrow room, with doorways at each end connecting to the hinter passage, but for some 100 years has been a pub. Underneath the bar is an ancient well, whilst the room above is reputedly haunted. Outside, a patio area annexes the car park, and there are tables and seats around the recently developed pond and lawn area. A range of meals is available in the bar or busy restaurant, whilst accommodation may also be obtained. The restaurant has been the village cinema, a cowshed, tea rooms and a bomb shelter during the last war.

The beers are very quaffable Pedigree and Tetley bitters, both delivered by handpump. An interesting item can be found just inside the side entrance, near the restaurant. A glass case contains a battered hat, which belonged to Alec Platt, and was sadly run over by a juggernaut. Presumably Alec was not wearing it at the time, for in his efforts to revive it by washing, the hat sadly passed away.

Open: Monday – Saturday, 11.30 – 2.30, 6.45 – 11; Sunday, 12 – 2.30, 7 – 10.30

Food: Bar snacks every lunchtime except Sunday. Restaurant each lunchtime and evening except Sunday night and Monday lunchtime.

The Hollybush

Breedon on the Hill

The hill at Breedon may only be 180 feet higher than the surrounding plain, but it is a landmark for many miles and an excellent viewpoint. Pleasant paths meander from the town below, through patches of gorse and violets in season.

It is mentioned as Briudun in the 7th century Anglo-Saxon Chronicle, its name deriving from *Bre* meaning "a hill" and dun also meaning "hill", in Welsh and Anglo-Saxon respectively. The importance of the rock is immediately apparent, the dolomite and limestone supporting the church on top being extensively quarried to the east and north.

It is not known for how long it has been inhabited, but a 3000 year old stone axe has been found in the vicinity. It still carries the remains of an Iron Age hill fort of the first centuery BC, traces of which are apparent even though most of it has disappeared into the quarry.

Parts of the present church, uniquely dedicated to St Mary and St Hardulph, date from the 12th century, added on to the original monastery of 675. Inside is a collection of Saxon sculpture, built into the church walls, which is the finest in England and different in style to anything else in Continental Europe. They are of the 8th and 9th centuries, depicting animals, people and geometrical patterns. A guide book may be purchased, giving more details and information, on this most attractive of churches. Other interesting features are the elegant medieval font, the monuments to the Shirley family, their monstrous 1627 pew and the neat box pews.

The town below includes a curious 18th century round house with a conical top and nail-studded door, once the village lock-up, apparently constructed out of old church stones.

Despite references to the contrary, Breedon is in Leicestershire and not Derbyshire, the latter being the postal address.

The Walk

1. From the Lime Kiln head right up the main road towards Castle Donington. After 150 metres turn left up The Delph, just before the old lock-up. After passing Ina's Cottage turn right up the gravel track, and as the road goes left downhill, fork upwards to the right. At the waymarkers keep going to the right and up until you emerge at the top, then continue to the church.

   In the graveyard, 25 metres south-east of the church, is the Swithland slate gravestone of John Johnson. He was the steward to the 4th Earl Ferrers, a son of the Shirley Family, and was murdered by Ferrers after refusing to falsely administer the trust fund for the Earl's separated wife. Ferrers was arrested and executed at Tyburn with the noble's "privilege" of a silken cord,

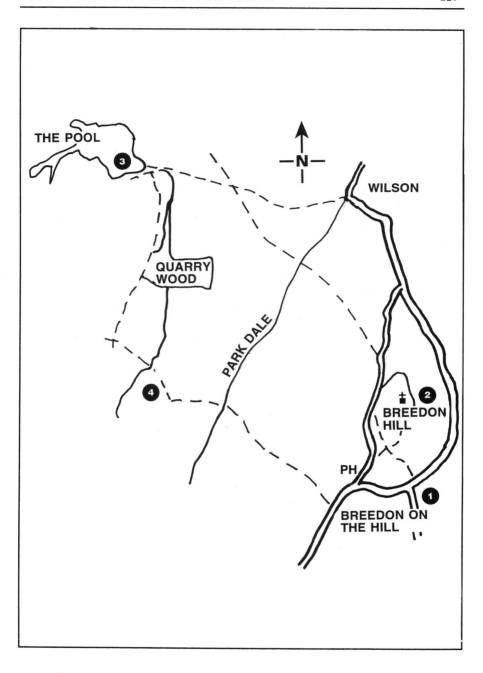

becoming the first man to try out the "new drop" and also the last peer of the realm to be hanged. The case was one of the most sensational murder trials of the 18th century, but sadly the inscription on Johnson's headstone tells none of the true story. Instead we learn only that he was the "esteem'd and faithful servant" of Shirley and the "incorruptible steward" of Ferrers before his "untimely death". Hushing up the truth with money is not a new phenomenon.

2. On leaving the church turn left to the car park, and then down the road. Just after the left-hand bend, take the footpath to the right signposted to Wilson. Go down to the road, turning right then left 100 metres later by the stile, waymarked to Melbourne. The path is well marked across the golf course, a line of yellow posts showing the way alongside some new trees. At the end cross the stile into the road, going straight across and through the gap in the hedge.

    The path heads over the field and to the right of the house opposite. Enter the lane, going right and then quickly left over a stile into Derbyshire. Head diagonally right down the field to the stile in the corner, going through the gate in front and down the farm road towards the wood. Pass through a gate, with the wall of Melbourne Hall to the right, and continue by the house. You meet a small gate on your left signposted Burney Lane 1, which you go through.

3. Alternatively a pleasant diversion is to continue down the track, turning right past The Pool and into the village. The hall used to be owned by the Lamb family, who took the name Melbourne as their peerage. Viscount Melbourne was the first Prime Minister of Queen Victoria, and she commemorated his name as the capital of the state named after her in Australia. Thomas Cook, of tourism fame, was also born here. There is a magnificent church, an interesting hall with justifiably famous gardens and a good selection of pubs. Unfortunately, as far as this book goes, it is not in Leicestershire, and so our walk does not actually include it.

    The path across the field is well trodden, and takes you alongside Quarry Wood. At the end of the field it drops down a bank and over a stile, reminiscent of a fence at the Badminton Horse Trials. Follow the barbed wire, passing through the right-hand of the three gates along a grassy tree-lined avenue from the hall. Continue through the next gate and turn immediately left in the direction indicated by the wooden signpost, that is diagonally across the field. A concrete v-shaped stile is met in line with the gaps in the trees, leading to a rather shaky footbridge and three more stiles going directly up the hill in front.

4. This leads into the middle of a field with no apparent path. The right of way goes straight across, and it is at moments like this that we appreciate the excellent yellow posts in Leicestershire. Unfortunately we are still in Derbyshire, so just aim for the crest of the hill, meeting a drain cover or personhole, from where you should see the v-stile in the hedge in front of you.

Go through the stile and over the ditch, turning right until a crossing hedge is met. Turn left just before it by a yellow marker, going down the mud path over the small stream in the copse. Emerge onto the wide grassy path by the right-hand hedge, and follow it to the road.

Turn left to the unusual war memorial, where you take the left fork to the Holly Bush Inn. On leaving go left, then right past Cherry Orchard. Turn right down Cross Street to the main road, where you will find the bus stop and further temptation in the form of the Lime Kiln Inn.

26. LONG WHATTON

Route: Long Whatton – Kegworth – Long Whatton

Distance: 6.5 miles, 10 kilometres. Good paths, quiet roads.

Map: O.S. Landranger 129 (Nottingham and Loughborough)

Start: All Saints Church, Long Whatton. Grid reference SK 482233

Access: Long Whatton lies off the A6, 5 miles north-west of Lough-borough. Frequent buses from Loughborough, Nottingham and Derby, including the Barton 3, Midland Fox 122, South Notts 121 and the Stevenson 177. Limited parking near the church.

Every author is allowed a little bias and self-indulgence, and I feel that I must declare that this walk has really been included because of the excellent pubs in Kegworth. The Cap and Stocking has for many years been a particular favourite with my football team, Hole in the Wall, whilst we have played in the area, whilst the Red Lion is a recent addition to the chain which includes the exceptional Lincolnshire Poacher in Nottingham. If time is short omit the walk rather than the pubs.

Cap and Stocking, Kegworth (0509 674814)

The present-day building dates back only to 1910, photographs in the bar show the then landlord and his customers, but there has probably been a pub here from Queen Elizabeth I's time. The name is unique, referring to the 17th century law in which everyone over the age of six had to wear a woollen cap on Sundays and Holy Days, and Borough Street was originally called Cap and Stocking Street. Its mixture of bars are all intimate and warmly furnished, with a collection of stuffed birds and fish from the early 20th century, many of which were caught by the landlord. Tastefully and sympathetically extended in the 1980s, it is an example to all breweries of what a pub should be like.

The beers include Bass from the jug, Highgate mild and a variety of guest ales. The food includes authentic Indian, Chinese and "exotic foods", with occasional theme evenings. Seats outside and a garden complete an excellent pub.

Open: Monday – Saturday, 11.30 – 3, 6 – 11; Sunday, 12 – 3, 7 – 10.30

Food: Monday – Saturday, 12 – 2.30, 6 – 9; Sunday, 12 – 2.30, 7 – 9

'Landlord' ale at the Cap and Stocking

Red Lion, Kegworth (0509 672466)

This Victorian addition to a Georgian house was formerly the Horse and Groom, and housed the local public toilets in its yard. It is very much a local, having associations with local teams and societies, its own racing pigeon, Flap, and a point-to-point racehorse. The rooms are unpretentiously furnished; a cosy lounge has a tiled floor, whilst the other two rooms are equally welcoming. Pictures of old Kegworth adorn the walls, whilst the sash windows in the bar have the initials of many previous landlords etched in their surroundings. There are plans to extend the lounge into a family dining area, when the catering will offer a variety of homecooked foods without chips at lunchtimes. Boddington, Marston, Tetley, Bass, M and B mild plus guest beers make up a formidable range, all of which are well-kept, and on Sunday lunchtime assorted nibbles are given away.

The pub had a Xmas party for its regulars on February 14th 1993, complete with decorations and crackers, and it is intended to make this an annual occurrence. Outside are seats, playground and garden with a small pets' corner. One resident is the 10 stone Irish wolfhound who demolished a 7lb haggis barbecued by the pub window cleaner – known as Porthole Pete because he only cleans the bit in the middle – which was left to cool in the dog run.

Open: Monday – Saturday, 11 – 3, 5 – 11; Sunday, 12 – 3, 7 – 10.30

Food: See above. Should be Monday – Saturday lunchtime.

Long Whatton

An aptly named village, stretching out along a central road with many interesting houses. The church of All Saints is an oddity, with its Norman tower being positioned at the east end of the south aisle rather than to the west. This arrangement was common in pre-conquest times, but is very rare nowadays in a small church and supposedly unique in Leicestershire. The chancel screen, brought in from the ruined church in Colston Bassett, Notts, is a good example of 15th century carving, whilst the churchyard contains many examples of the Swithland slate tombstone. Here is buried Aaron Boswell, a gypsy, whose possessions were destroyed, burned or broken and buried, according to the Romany customs.

The two pubs are well worth a visit; the Falcon serving Everard's beers will be met on our walk, and the Royal Oak to the east of the church serves Marston's.

The Walk

1. From the church turn right down Mill Lane, with its attractive cottages, crossing the Long Whatton Brook that runs parallel to the village. Note on your right a decaying concrete footpath raised above the road, a common sight in these flood-susceptible areas. When the road bends sharply to the right, go straight on through a gate by a footpath sign. Keep by the hedge, and when it ends follow the arrow across the next field to a tractor path. Carry on up the lane to the right of the woodland and climb a stile in front of you.

2. Aim diagonally left to the corner of the field, mounting the fence by a waymarker. Keep by the hedge at the field side as the view, marred by Ratcliffe Power Station, opens up in front of you. Head down to Slade Farm, turning right with the field edge, then left through an old gate, before going across to the farm fence. Turn right at the fence and proceed to the farm road, where you turn left then right along the edge of the copse. Follow the path by the right of the hedge and go down to the concrete footbridge.

   The spire of Kegworth church is directly in front of you, indeed this path is part of an ancient way linking the Trent Valley with Charnwood Forest. A perusal of the map shows that the churches of Kegworth, Long Whatton, Shepshed and Bardon Hill are virtually in a straight line.

3. Cross the bridge, and continue along the obvious path besides the butchered hedgerow. Perhaps the newly planted wood to your right will help compensate the wildlife. When you meet a track turn right along it to the main road, turning left to the centre of Kegworth.

   Kegworth was a medieval market town and later a thriving centre for framework knitting. Some interesting houses lie in the vicinity of the Brittania Inn, including an old knitters' workshop, with the large dormer windows.

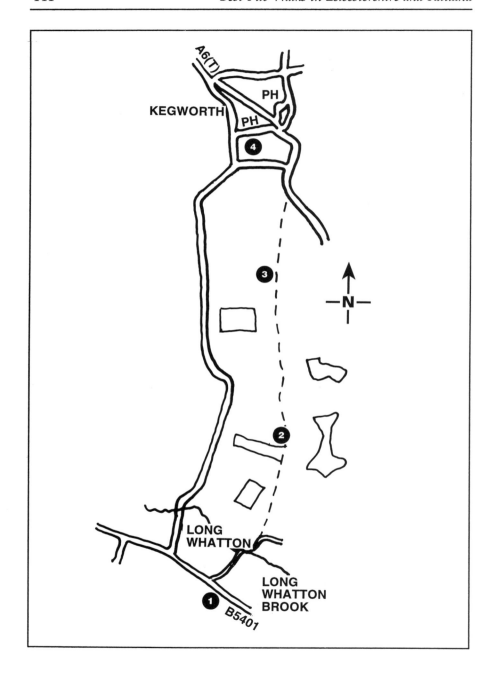

Thomas Moore, the poet, lived in the Cedars on London Road, and John Kirk, who was fundamental in the setting up of the Ragged Schools for poor children, was born in a house opposite the church.

Cross the busy A6 by the pedestrian lights and enter the church of St Andrew. Although it contains nothing of outstanding merit, it is a pleasing and dignified building. On leaving turn right up Market Place, then left down the hill on London Road. As you reach the playing fields turn left into Borough Street, and follow it round left into the welcoming embrace of the Cap and Stocking. Suitably refreshed, continue up the hill, following the road as it narrows and turns left. At the main road go left, cross at the lights and then go up High Street to your right. The Red Lion is situated 100 metres down on the right-hand side.

4. With a little more of a roll to your gait, continue along the High Street, turning left up Broadhill Road and then right along Whatton Road. This quiet lane is followed for the next 4 kilometres into Long Whatton, an eminently practical route after what may have been a long visit to two such excellent pubs. Ahead Charnwood Forest can be seen, an attractive vista across the undulating countryside.

The lane joins the main road at Long Whatton by the Falcon, where you turn left. On the left-hand side Keeper's Cottage, number 61, is a picturesque late 16th century dwelling, and other houses of interest are passed on the way back to the church.

27. CASTLE DONINGTON

Route: Castle Donington – Hemington – Lockington – Castle Donington.

Distance: 4 miles, 6.5 kilometres. Well defined paths, minor roads out of Donington.

Map: O.S. Landranger 129 (Nottingham and Loughborough)

Start: Bus station, Castle Donington. Grid reference SK 444273.

Access: Frequent buses from Derby, Loughborough, Ashby and Nottingham. Car parking is possible in the town, but not at the bus station.

Jolly Sailor, Hemington (0332 810448)

An unusually shaped pub, set back from the road, serving a wide range of real ales including Bass, Pedigree, M and B mild and a real cider, with three other guest beers. A long bar serves both sections, with the less formal side featuring an interesting collection of brass blowlamps. This pub caters for the discerning drinker and is worth an extended visit, which given that it opens all day is quite a likely occurrence. There are seats outside for those fine summer evenings.

Open: Monday – Saturday, 11 – 11; Sunday, 12 – 3, 7 – 10.30

Food: None at present.

Castle Donington

An old town perched proudly on the hill side, with imposing views into the Trent Valley. The nearby East Midlands Airport and Donington Park Motor Racing Circuit can bring a disproportionate amount of traffic and noise at certain times of the year, particularly during the "Monsters of Rock" concerts, but the town itself still retains a pleasant and peaceful centre with many interesting buildings.

The castle has long since disappeared, destroyed by its owner in 1595 when he built the Hall, but the houses in the vicinity contain many of the old stones in their walls. The moat is still obvious in the steep banked gardens.

The church of Edward, King and Martyr is now usually locked, but if you arrive around the time of a service then you may glimpse the monuments and brasses that are of import.

An old village term, still in use today, is that of Eastwinders, used to denote newcomers to the village. The term is believed to date back to the times when invaders from the Continent would use the east wind to cross the North Sea and sail up the Trent. Should you be looking for a pub, we recommend the Cross Keys on the main B6540, down the hill from the bus station.

The Jolly Sailor

The Walk

1. From the bus station, go to the lights and then right down the hill past the Donington Manor Hotel. Turn right opposite the Moira Arms, and go up Market Street to the town centre. On your right an iron gateway leads up a yew-fringed path to the church, the resting place of Ferdinando Hastinges, whose inscription reads:

   Ferdinando Hastinges
   Of God he stands in fear
   Is of his name
   The anagram
   So of his pious mind
   The happy character

   Unfortunately the anagram is not correct, but the sentiment no doubt suited this 17th century son of the Earl of Huntingdon whose family owned the Hall.

   Return to the road, turn right, and at the Give Way sign continue across past the church up Castle Hill.

2. A short wander among the houses gives some idea of where the castle was situated, but sadly they block the view over the surrounding countryside. Part of the castle cellars remain inside Castle House, as does an old fireplace. Go back to the main road and turn right past the Jolly Potter down Hillside.

3. As the main road is reached, a sign on the right indicates the footpath along which we walk between two old hedgerows. Pass a tree-shrouded spring, cross a stile and continue straight on along the obvious path at the foot of the hill. After going under some electricity cables head slightly right uphill with the path joining a surfaced path by a gate onto the road.

   Turn left and go past the war memorial to the Three Horseshoes. From there continue left down the road and into the Jolly Sailor. Return to the war memorial and take the left-hand fork past the Nunnery, an 18th century block of lodgings that were formerly joined to Hemington Hall, and had nothing to do with nuns at all. The hall itself can be glimpsed later on, a

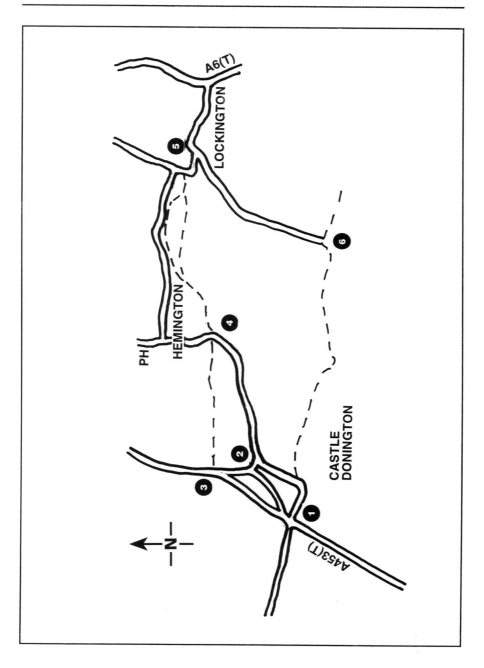

13th century building much extended and rebuilt by the Harpur family, whose name lives on in the pub name of Crewe and Harpur I believe.

4. Take the footpath to the left through a gate and pass alongside the ruined church, a 13th century building that has been disused since the 16th century. Little remains now, but the ivy-shrouded and jackdaw covered tower presents a pretty picture. Continue along the obvious path as it bends right, with earthworks and trenches from the attack on the hall during the Civil War on the hill above.

Continue through a kissing gate and slightly uphill along the path. This is a well-worn groove, no doubt centuries old and presumably the old road between Hemington and Lockington. Go through a gate and head towards a right-hand fence before descending into the village. Ahead looms the Ratcliffe Power Station, aficionados may debate as to whether or not its beauty outstrips that of the one at Donington, looming behind us.

Go through two more gates, turn left at the road and then quickly right down a narrow lane to the church of St Nicholas.

5. To your left the 17th century Lockington Hall, now a business centre, hides behind the trees as you enter the churchyard. Sadly this church is also locked, although a Saxon stone in the porch may be seen.

One of its former rectors, Reverend Robert Laycock, is famous for having shot the last brace of grouse in Charnwood Forest during the late 19th century. He was also a passionate fan of cockfighting, breeding birds to match against those of the Marquis of Hastings. Reputedly they even conducted one contest among the church pews during a Sunday service.

From the porch turn right and take the short path to the main road that bends around the churchyard, much to the discomfort of motorists. Go down the road to the T-junction, turning left up Main Street past an imposingly-tall farmhouse. As the road turns right, continue past the metal barrier up the signposted bridlepath to the side of the wood known as The Dumps. After a kilometre turn right by a footpath sign just over the brow of the hill.

6. Follow the obvious tractor route, climbing over an iron pole onto a footpath in the next field. Keep with the path as it heads to the clump of trees, picking up another tractor track which becomes concrete.

Cross a stile by a gate, leaving the lane, which is not a right of way, and follow the path near to the left-hand hedge to a second stile. Turn right along the road, then after 50 metres head left along a prominent mud path which is not signposted. Continue along this, skirting the edge of a football pitch, and emerge through a gap in the houses onto a road. Go straight down Eastway, turn left at the junction by the school and then right along Mount Pleasant to the bus station.

Cottages at Hemington

28. SCALFORD

Route: Scalford – Goadby Marwood – Scalford

Distance: 3.8 miles, 6 kilometres. Good path, quiet lanes.

Map: O.S. Landranger 129 (Nottingham and Loughborough)

Start: Scalford Church. Grid reference SK 763242

Access: Scalford is 4 miles north of Melton Mowbray. The infrequent Barton 2 and Fairtax 5, both Melton to Bottesford, stop near to the church. Car parking is possible in the village.

The Kings Arms, Scalford (0664 76208)

The comfortable lounge serves Pedigree, John Smith's and Directors bitters. A good selection of food is available, either in the bar or the restaurant. The lounge is intimate, furnished with point-to point photographs, whilst behind is a small open-plan public and corridor drinking area, the notorious Tramps bar, where the local farmers gather. Upstairs is a large restaurant seating 42 people, serving a variety of homecooked dishes including "Old Tom" steak and kidney pie. There are tables outside at the rear, and a garden area.

Open: Monday – Saturday, 11 – 2.30, 7 – 11; Sunday, 12 – 2.30, 7 – 10.30

Food: 12 – 1.45, 7 – 9.45

Scalford

A tidy village built around the church of St Egelwine, the only church in England dedicated to this saint. He was the brother of Kenwalch, King of the West Saxons in the 7th century, and is thought to be buried here. The churchyard contains a fragment of the ancient village cross, but it is the large south porch that catches the eye. Formerly it was two storeys high and contained statues in the recesses.

The dairy here produces 100 prize-winning Stilton Cheeses each day, but the brickyard that once employed over 100 people has disappeared. One former resident of Scalford was Colonel Colman of mustard fame, whilst another, William ''Peppermint Billy'' Brown was the last person to be executed in public at Leicester Prison, in 1856.

The village stands on the Jubilee Way, a fifteen and a half mile walk from Melton to Woolsthorpe, near Belvoir.

The Walk

1. Leave the churchyard by the path to the north, on the opposite side to the porch and cross. Turn left up the hill, then right along Sandy Lane by the signpost to the village hall. Cross the car park and the football pitch aiming for a bridge and stile with attendant yellow Jubilee Way sign (J.W.). The arrow points the way along the path to the gate in the corner, where a grassy tractor route is picked up. Continue over a bridge and turn right and then left along the field edge.

   Go past some old LWD mains signs, your guess as to the meaning is as good as ours and we settled on Leicestershire Water Department. The path then goes between the supports of a dismantled railway, once used to carry iron ore, and it continues straight on but with the hedge now on your left.

   To the right the transmitter near Waltham on the Wolds is prominent, as you go over a stile and head downhill to a bridge over Scalford Brook. Turn left alongside a small spinney, the willows of which have now grown too large for their use in the making of cricket bats, and head slightly uphill to a gate.

2. Keep alongside the wood, and when it turns to the right go left by a marker down to a stile. Aim diagonally across the field to the right-hand edge of the hawthorn hedge, where you follow the J.W. marker and fence to your left. When you meet the old wall of Goadby Hall, turn right along the deeply rutted track. Pass through a gate, and then turn left as a lane joins from the right. We will return to this point later, so make a mental note of it.

   Continue along the lane towards Goadby Marwood, with the hall prominent in the view, turning right and then left with the road by a strange outbuilding of the hall, a Gothic Victorian lodge cum estate house made to look like a chapel. At the bottom go through the gate and into the churchyard of St Denys.

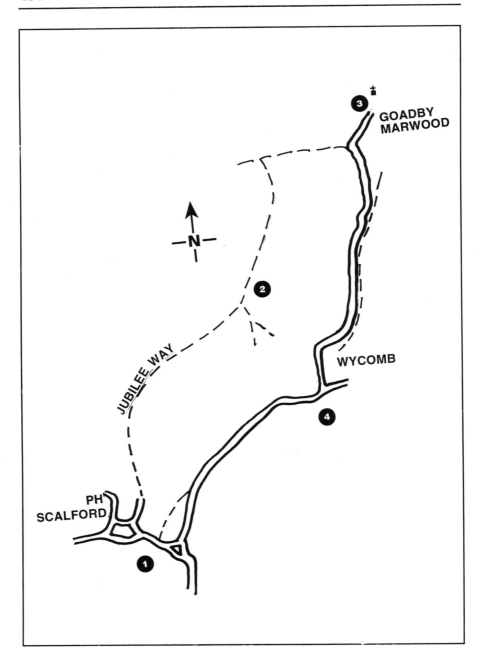

3. This 13th century church is not of exceptional merit, but contains much of interest. Inside a display case contains objects found locally of both Roman and medieval origin, confirming that the area around was a Roman market and industrial centre. There is a wall monument to the Maureward, Beaumont and Villiers families who owned the hall between 1300 and 1680, and in the north wall of the chancel the following inscription about Peter Wyche who died in 1763 may be found:

Reader
immitate his virtues and forget his Faults
His Virtues were such as rendered him
usefull to Society, beneficial to Mankind
and happy in himself.
His Faults, whether Publick or Private
were Such as fully prov'd
the frailty of Human Nature
to be the Source of Human errors.
As he lived, So he died.
An Example worthy of imitation

One of the rectors here was Edmund Cartwright, whose invention of the power loom radically altered industrial life, not only for Leicestershire but for the whole of the North of England. The churchyard is sadly overgrown at the rear, but contains a glorious display of snowdrops in season.

Return up the lane towards Scalford, going right in front of the "lodge", left soon after and then after 100 metres take the metaled road left towards Wycomb Cottage, now renamed the White House. The road is then followed for about a mile to Wycomb, a quiet publess village boasting a thriving monkey puzzle tree.

4. At the main road, turn right down a quiet road with good grass verges. We go under the old railway, pass a shooting range, and as the road bends left, turn right by the footpath sign and over a stile.

Keep to the top edge of the bank above the stream, ignoring the footbridge down below. When you meet a crossing hedge climb the fence, then drop slowly down the bank, heading towards the fence where the brook meets the road. Turn right past the Dairy to the church, where the right-hand fork leads to the Kings Arms and the left-hand one to the Plough, a recently renovated pub serving the range of Theakstone's beers.

29. BELVOIR

Route: Knipton – Wolsthorpe – Belvoir – Knipton

Distance: 6.9 miles, 11 kilometres. Some roads can be busy in summer, so not very suitable for small children.

Map: O.S. Landranger 130 Grantham

Start: Knipton Village, by the pump. Grid reference SK 825313

Access: Knipton lies between Melton and Grantham, just south of Belvoir Castle. By bus, the infrequent Skinner 2 Grantham to Eaton, and Lincolnshire Road Car 605 Grantham to Harston only give limited access. Several coach firms do trips to Belvoir Castle, and the walk may be undertaken from there. Car parking is possible in Knipton or at Belvoir.

Red House, Knipton (0476 870352)

This lovely old Georgian hotel is situated in open land with exceptional views and a most restful beer garden. There is a conservatory extension to the restaurant, or you may eat in the high-ceilinged bar. This is split into two areas by a wide fireplace, the lounge side being adorned by hunting pictures of Prince Charles, whilst the more homely public section has a dart board. The Tetley and Burton bitters may be enjoyed in either.

It is haunted by the ghost of a little girl, which has been seen by the landlady. Accommodation is available, and there are a variety of animals including pot-bellied pigs and an aviary outside.

Open: Monday – Saturday, 11 – 3, 6 – 11; Sunday, 12 – 3, 7 – 10.30

Food: 12 – 2, 7 – 10

Belvoir

The name derives from the French for beautiful view, and dates back to Norman times. The first castle was built in the 11th century by Robert de Todeni, Standard Bearer to William the Conquerer at the Battle of Hastings, but the present building dates mainly from the early 19th century. Its situation is peerless in the county, and its towers, turrets and crenellations make it the epitome of a fairytale castle.

The Manners family have been the owners since the 15th century, and the impressive 19th century mausoleum contains the tombs of the latter Dukes of Rutland; their predecessors being in Bottesford Church. Also in the grounds are seven statues c. 1680 by Cibber on the terraces, and a Temple and Grotto in the Spring Gardens.

Inside, the castle contains two Picture Galleries, a range of ornate Saloons and the 17th/21st Lancers museum. The chapel houses the tomb of de Todeni, who was also the founder of the Priory that lies mainly buried at the foot of Blackberry Hill.

The castle is open from Easter to October, on Wednesdays, Thursdays, Saturdays and Sundays plus Bank Holidays. Many special events are held, including the popular jousting tournaments, and a visit combined with the walk makes for an enjoyable and full day out.

The Walk

1. From the pump and its shelter, turn right along the main road towards Harston, taking the first turn right by the signboard to the Red House. Return to the road, turning right along Pasture Lane for the mile to Harston. Good views of the castle may be had, and the Belvoir Sports Ground will be met. At the top of the hill on the fringes of Harston, turn right up a narrow unmarked path between tall hedges, just after the rectory. This leads to the church, which although largely rebuilt is nevertheless worth visiting for the well-kept gardens, the view and the Saxon lattice stone embedded in the porch. On leaving the churchyard follow the gravel path to the road, where you turn left and then right towards Denton.

2. After 800 metres turn left up Sewstern Lane, once the main road from

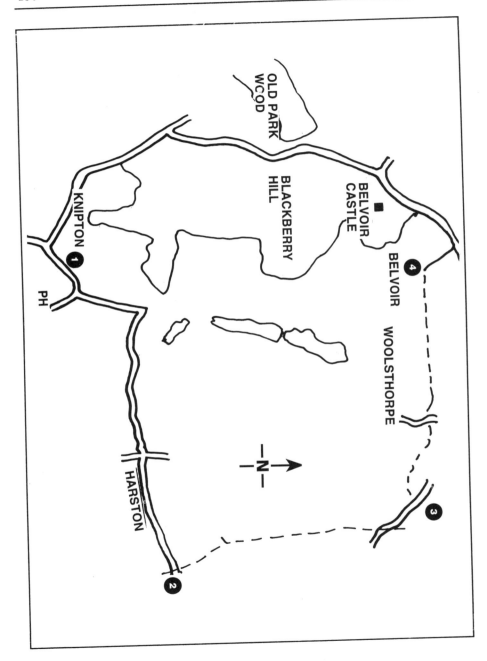

Stanford to York and now part of the Viking Way (V.W.). More details can be found in the Bottesford Walk. A V.W. sign is met shortly after New Cottages, with their allotment-style gardens, and you then cross over a disused railway. Continue up the obvious old lane and pass into Lincolnshire.

The main road is met at a place called Brewers Grave, reputedly the burial site of a brewer from the castle who drowned in a vat of beer. Legend also states that his donkey is buried beside him, but whether or not he was riding it when he drowned is not recorded. They must have had some wild parties in those days.

To the left is an ornate gateway leading onto an old avenue to the castle. It is not a right of way, so please continue, turning slightly left down the road. Pass the lodge and leave the V.W., which continues up the old dirt road, and go by the side of the wood. After 200 metres a gate and ruined stile are found on your left, and you go through and up the road to the private tip. Just before the tip climb a gate on your left adorned with Jubilee Way (J.W.) markers and arrows. Turn right along the edge of the wood, with the open parkland in front of you.

As the wood turns right, head straight downhill towards a shed. Stop to admire the view. There, wasn't that worth it? There is a stile in front of the shed, and after climbing the stile you find out that the shed is in fact a scorebox for the cricket club. Go left around the outfield, passing a J.W. marker, to emerge onto a car park for a deceased pub.

At the main road turn left and then right up Belvoir Lane, at the end of which you cross the bridge back into Leicestershire. Climb the stile and take the path by the hedge in front of you. Occasionally kerb stones can be seen, indicating that this was once a driveway to the castle, and a further stile is crossed.

4. At a Private sign go right, passing a J.W. marker and redundant stile. The path is followed to the road where you turn left. The road can be busy in summer, so please take care and use the verges wherever possible. Pass the car park, taking the left-hand fork to Knipton. The large field to your right is called the West Wong, a wong being a measure of land equivalent to a furlong in Norse times.

There is plenty of room to the side of the road, but when the road bends to the right and the J.W. way turns off more care is needed. Continue down the road, with the view opening out to the left down to the small lake in Frog Hollow. At the junction turn left, heading downhill into Knipton.

In the village take the right-hand road up Church Hill to the church of All Saints, a mainly 13th century building. In the whitewashed interior can be found some attractive stained glass and a memorial to a small child, sculpted in swaddling clothes, bearing the inscription

"Off your charite praye for the soule of john eyre
son of cristofer eyre, gent, whiche ded the viiii
daye of aprill in the yere of our lord god
mccccclviii" (1558)

Return to the road, turning right to our starting point and perhaps a reunion with the Red House.

30. BOTTESFORD

Route: Bottesford – Muston – Bottesford

Distance: 8.8 miles, 14 kilometres. Old grassy tracks, good paths.

Map: O.S. Landranger 130 (Grantham)

Start: Market Cross, Market Street. Grid reference SK 487389

Access: Bottesford is just off the A52, 6 miles west of Grantham. Frequent trains on the Nottingham to Grantham line give easy access, and there are less frequent buses such as the Barton's 2, from Melton via Vale of Belvoir, and the Lincolnshire Road Company 55 and X6 from Bingham or Grantham. Car parking is possible in the village or by the station.

The Bull Inn, Bottesford (0949 42288)

A low-ceilinged 18th century inn which was once kept by the sister of Stan Laurel of Laurel and Hardy fame. They stayed here in 1953 whilst appearing at the theatre in Nottingham for a season. The good quality Home Ales are delivered by electric pump, but taste none the worse for that, and there is also Theakston's XB.

The popular public bar is divided into three sections, with a log fire in one part. The pool room part may be used by children in the early evening.

Open: Monday – Friday, 11.30 – 2.30, 5.30 – 11; Saturday, 11.30 – 4, 7 – 11; Sunday, 12 – 3, 7 – 10.30

Food: Cobs only at Saturday lunchtime.

Bottesford

This large village has an attractive core, particularly in the vicinity of the churchyard and River Devon. The stump of the 600-year-old market cross is complemented by ancient stocks, and the surrounding buildings from the 16th century onwards show a variety of styles and materials, with the red pantiled roofs a common feature.

The gem of the village is St Mary's Church, with its 210 feet high spire, the highest in the county for a parish church and a noted landmark. Inside are monuments to the Roos and Manners families, the Dukes of Rutland whose descendants still own Belvoir Castle.

An excellent guidebook gives details of the fascinating interior, with a medieval wall painting, a nationally important brass from 1404 and the various tombs displaying 400 years of stonemasonry. The brass is hidden beneath a carpet to protect it from wear, but it is allowable to lift up the covering to view it or even take a rubbing for a fee.

Perhaps the most famous tomb is that of Francis, the 6th Earl, which is believed to be the only monument in the country to refer to people killed by sorcery. Joan Flower and her daughters were convicted of murdering the Earl's children by witchcraft, in revenge for Margaret Flower being dismissed from employment at the castle. Joan asked for some bread and butter to prove her innocence as "she wished it would never go through her if she was guilty". On tasting it she promptly dropped down dead, presumably by self-administered poison, but it certainly did her daughters no favour as it sealed their guilt and they were hanged in Lincoln in 1618.

Two other stone carvings are by Grinling Gibbons, more famous as a woodcarver, whilst others have been brought here from the long vanished Croxton Abbey and Belvoir Priory. An hour spent in this most interesting of churches is amply repaid.

The Walk

1. Proceed from the cross past the Red Lion along Grantham Road, turning left down St Mary's Lane, now a footpath. At the end go right over Fleming's Bridge, built by a rector in the early 17th century, and enter the churchyard.

    After leaving the church turn right, and then go through an iron kissing gate onto a footpath. Turn right and continue past side turnings to the end, where you turn left along a path with a pond to the right. At the road continue roughly straight ahead, by the bridlepath sign and over the level crossing.

    Go up the grassy lane, turning right after 100 metres by a footpath sign and map. Take the path through the hedge to Allington, aiming diagonally to the left on the path thoughtfully and carefully reinstated each year by a considerate farmer. Continue past the corner of a hedge until meeting a cross-hedge by a blue marker. Turn right, go through a gate and follow the obvious track by the right-hand hedge. This becomes a grassy lane at a marker which we follow to a second post.

2. Here the marked route goes across the field, but the farmer has laid out an alternate path up the wide grassy strip to your right and it would seem to be only courteous to use it. Turn left at the top, then right by a ditch, followed by a quick left-right as signed. To your right the old road is overgrown by the hedgerow, but we soon join it as the farm path from Debdale Barn crosses our way. Ignore the signposted bridlepath to the left and follow the track between the hedges, the overgrown hawthorn on your left contrasting with the well pruned one to your right at the field boundary.

    The path turns right, and can be chewed up in places, but as it turns left it opens out into an excellent wide lane. We now slip temporarily into Lincolnshire to make use of the old roads, and to appreciate the extensive views to the north. When another grassy road crosses ours we turn right, passing a Viking Way sign and yellow marker, up a track unsuitable for motorists.

    The Viking Way is a long distance footpath from the Humber Bridge to Oakham, about 120 miles in length. The part we are now on is the ancient Sewstern Lane or The Drift, which may date from the Bronze Age. It was at one time the main route from the Trent to Stamford, but it gradually became

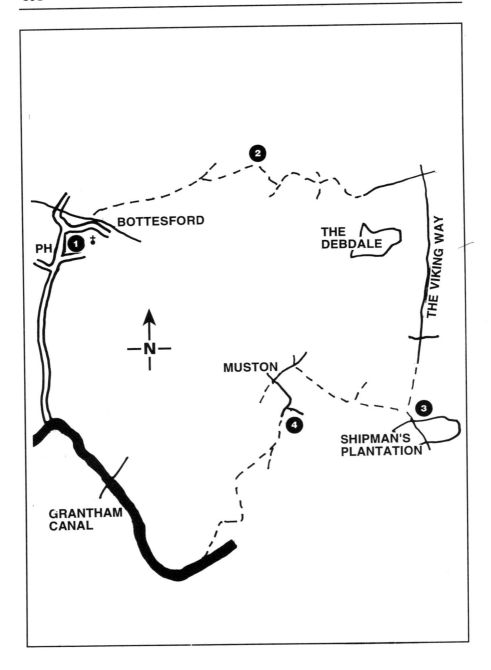

less important and ended up as a drove road for cattle and sheep which gave it its name. It makes you wonder what the nearby A1 will look like in a couple of thousand years; not so good I imagine.

Continue down the lane for 2 kilometres, crossing the railway and the A52. To the right Bottesford spire stands out like a dagger thrusting against the skyline, whilst in front of you Belvoir Castle becomes more obvious on the tree-clad ridge. Go up the metalled road opposite, past Mill Farm Cottages and then the newer Mill Farm.

3. As the road turns to the left, leave the Viking Way by turning right along the tractor path in front of the derelict house. Pass the old decaying Mill Farm buildings and keep with the track to the bridge over the stream. Turn right just before the stream along the field edge, a faint path and hoofprints leading the way.

The path follows the meandering river before turning right at the end of the field. 80 metres later turn left just before the start of the hedge, crossing the old railway line to the Belvoir Quarries. Cross the stile and aim slightly right towards the spire of Muston church. Enter the churchyard of St John the Baptist by a stile. Inside can be found a memorial to Sarah Crabbe, wife of the poet George Crabbe, who was rector here.

Go left at the road, then left again at the junction along Woolsthorpe Lane. You pass by the village cross on the green, rebuilt to mark the coronation of George V, before turning right at the end of the village along a bridlepath, the sign for which is just after Grener Norman Farm.

4. Go down the track through a couple of bends for about 1 kilometre, taking the left-hand fork at the end by the small copse beyond the metal gate. This track keeps by the edge of the field, passing a pylon until it turns right near the woodland at the end of the field. The route onto the canal towpath via the plank is not a right of way, so resist temptation and continue by the field edge. Turn left through a gap in the hedge, and follow the track to its end, where a left turn takes you to the canal.

Head right along the towpath, where you soon pass a post telling you that you are 25.5 miles from the Trent. This canal is the Grantham Canal, which leads to Nottingham. Extensive renovations have been carried out, but unfortunately, because many bridges have been removed, it will be a lengthy and costly process to restore it to working order. Many sections have been cleared of weeds and rubbish, and the towpath has been lovingly maintained with informative signs a bonus.

Pass what was bridge 56, and a stone hut. The canal bends left through a cutting, and we turn right at bridge 55 to leave the canal by the quaintly named Thisisit, now a kennels. Take the road to Bottesford, carefully crossing the A52, and pass the sports fields to arrive at the town centre near to the Bull Inn.

We publish a wide range of titles, including general interest publications, guides to individual towns, and books for outdoor activities centred on walking and cycling in the great outdoors throughout England and Wales. This is a recent selection:

Cycling with Sigma ...

CYCLE UK! The definitive guide to leisure cycling
– Les Lumsdon *(£9.95)*

OFF-BEAT CYCLING & MOUNTAIN BIKING IN THE PEAK DISTRICT
– Clive Smith *(£6.95)*

MORE OFF-BEAT CYCLING IN THE PEAK DISTRICT
– Clive Smith *(£6.95)*

50 BEST CYCLE RIDES IN CHESHIRE
– edited by Graham Beech *(£7.95)*

CYCLING IN THE LAKE DISTRICT
– John Wood *(£7.95)*

CYCLING IN SOUTH WALES
– Rosemary Evans *(£7.95)*

BY-WAY BIKING IN THE CHILTERNS
– Henry Tindell *(£7.95)*i

Books of Walks

There are many books for outdoor people in our catalogue, including:

RAMBLES IN NORTH WALES
– Roger Redfern

HERITAGE WALKS IN THE PEAK DISTRICT
– Clive Price

EAST CHESHIRE WALKS
– Graham Beech

WEST CHESHIRE WALKS
– Jen Darling

WEST PENNINE WALKS
– Mike Cresswell

STAFFORDSHIRE WALKS
– Les Lumsdon

NEWARK AND SHERWOOD RAMBLES
– Malcolm McKenzie

NORTH NOTTINGHAMSHIRE RAMBLES
– MAlcolm McKenzie

RAMBLES AROUND NOTTINGHAM & DERBY
– Keith Taylor

RAMBLES AROUND MANCHESTER
– Mike Cresswell

WESTERN LAKELAND RAMBLES
– Gordon Brown

WELSH WALKS:
Dolgellau and the Cambrian Coast
– Laurence Main and Morag Perrott

WELSH WALKS:
Aberystwyth and District
– Laurence Main and Morag Perrott

MOSTLY DOWNHILL:
Leisurely walks in the Lake District
– Alan Pears

WEST PENNINE WALKS
– Mike Cresswell

– all of the above books are currently £6.95 each

CHALLENGING WALKS IN NORTH-WEST BRITAIN
– Ron Astley *(£9.95)*

WALKING PEAKLAND TRACKWAYS
– Mike Cresswell *(£7.95)*

Long-distance walks:

For long-distance walks enthusiasts, we have several books including:

THE GREATER MANCHESTER BOUNDARY WALK – Graham Phythian

THE THIRLMERE WAY – Tim Cappelli

THE FURNESS TRAIL – Tim Cappelli

THE MARCHES WAY – Les Lumsdon

THE TWO ROSES WAY – Peter Billington, Eric Slater,
Bill Greenwood and Clive Edwards

THE RED ROSE WALK – Tom Schofield

FROM WHARFEDALE TO WESTMORLAND:
Historical walks through the Yorkshire Dales – Aline Watson

THE WEST YORKSHIRE WAY – Nicholas Parrott

– all £6.95 each

The Best Pub Walks!

Sigma publish the widest range of "Pub Walks" guides, covering just about every popular walking destination in England and Wales. Each book includes 25 – 30 interesting walks and varied suitable for individuals or family groups. *The walks are based on "Real Ale" inns of character and are all accessible by public transport.*

Areas covered include

Cheshire • Dartmoor • Exmoor • Isle of Wight • Yorkshire Dales • Peak District • Lake District • Cotswolds • Mendips • Cornwall • Lancashire • Oxfordshire • Snowdonia • Devon

… and dozens more – all £6.95 each!

General interest:

THE INCREDIBLY BIASED BEER GUIDE – Ruth Herman
This is the most comprehensive guide to Britain's smaller breweries and the pubs where you can sample their products. Produced with the collaboration of the Small Independent Brewers' Association and including a half-price subscription to The Beer Lovers' Club. £6.95

DIAL 999 – EMERGENCY SERVICES IN ACTION – John Creighton
Re-live the excitement as fire engines rush to disasters. See dramatic rescues on land and sea. Read how the professionals keep a clear head and swing into action. £9.95

THE ALABAMA AFFAIR – David Hollett
This is an account of Britain's rôle in the American Civil War. Read how Merseyside dockyards supplied ships for the Confederate navy, thereby supporting the slave trade. The *Alabama* was the most famous of the 'Laird Rams', and was chased half way across the world before being sunk ignominiously. £9.95

PEAK DISTRICT DIARY – Roger Redfern
An evocative book, celebrating the glorious countryside of the Peak District. The book is based on Roger's popular column in *The Guardian* newspaper and is profusely illustrated with stunning photographs. £6.95

I REMAIN, YOUR SON JACK – J. C. Morten (edited by Sheila Morten)
A collection of almost 200 letters, as featured on BBC TV, telling the moving story of a young soldier in the First World War. Profusely illustrated with contemporary photographs. £8.95